The Coconut
Latitudes

For Eileen
Thanks!

Rita Gardner

Published 2014

Printed in the United States of America
ISBN: 978-1-63152-901-6
Library of Congress Control Number: 2014935216

Book design by Stacey Aaronson
Map of the Dominican Republic by Mike Morgenfeld

For information, address:
She Writes Press
1563 Solano Ave #546
Berkeley, CA 94707

The Coconut Latitudes

Secrets, Storms, and Survival in the Caribbean

Rita M. Gardner

SHE WRITES PRESS

To my family

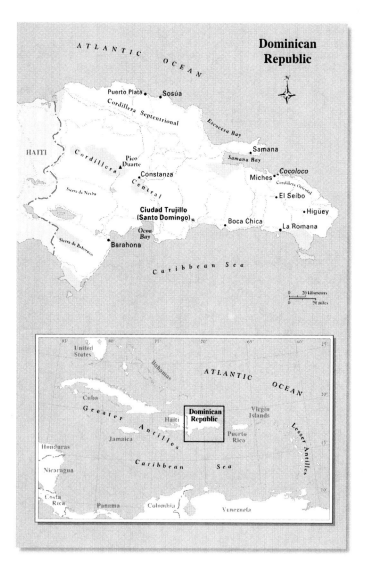

Introduction

❊

Before I am born, my father, for reasons shrouded in mystery, abruptly leaves a successful engineering career in the United States. He buys two hundred and fifty acres of remote beachfront land on Samana Bay in the Dominican Republic. This small, Spanish-speaking nation occupies two-thirds of the island of Hispaniola and is ruled by the dictator Rafael Trujillo. Haiti occupies the western third of the landmass. Trade winds blow year round all the way from the deserts in Africa, combing through palm groves and shaping the trunks into inverted commas. The island is also in the main path of hurricanes that storm through the Atlantic and Caribbean from June through November. In 1946, when I am six weeks old and my sister Berta is four, my father moves us into this instability. Our family lands—with a pile of suitcases, a box of books, and bright Fiesta dinnerware—years before there will be electric power or actual roads to Miches, the closest village.

At this time, access to our property is a four-hour boat trip from another town, or a daylong horseback ride over the *Cordillera Oriental* range. These mountains, my father says, will protect our land from the worst hurricanes. He hires a crew to plant ten thousand coconut seedlings and names the property Cocoloco Plantation. It will take several years for the palms to begin producing nuts. During that waiting period, he contracts with his former employer and the family sometimes travels with him to job sites around the globe.

When I'm five, we settle permanently in the small fishing village of Miches, four kilometers from our coconut *finca*. *Finca* is the Spanish word for farm, and dozens of such plantations stretch for miles along the empty shoreline on either side of town. My father originally joined with another American engineer on a larger parcel, but soon after the purchase, the partnership blew up and the land was divided. The family visits their *finca* frequently, and this is awkward since Berta and I are forbidden to speak to their children, a boy and a girl our same ages. It's not easy to ignore them when they are right next door, but Daddy plants a high hedge of hibiscus between our properties so we can't see their house. My mother goes along with whatever Daddy decides.

Other than the family we can't talk to, we will be the only English-speaking people within a hundred kilometers. My father frequently says we are a *damn* happy family; we've arrived in paradise, and are the luckiest people in the world.

"Islands . . . seem to take revenge on those who regard them as solutions or personal Edens."

—*Alastair Reid*

Chapter One

❋

Miches

It's a sticky summer day when we first bounce over the mountain in a ratty jeep driven by an old man with brown leather skin. The windshield is cracked and dust covers everything. Our suitcases are piled on top, strapped down by frayed ropes. We're not tied down by anything at all. We heave left and right as the jeep straddles the track that's barely a road. I'm used to these raggedy roads in the Dominican Republic— riding in a vehicle is always clattery and bumpy on this island.

Daddy sits up front with the driver, and in the smelly backseat, Mama wedges in between my sister Berta and me, trying to hold on to us as we lurch up yet another switchback. Berta turns white, leans out the window, and throws up. Daddy mumbles something about how since she's nine, she should be used to this by now and not get sick. The vehicle stops and I get sick too. Daddy tries to distract us by showing us a waterfall off in the distance, but all I can see is the mess I've made of my clothes. We pile in again and rumble onward, slowing down behind a donkey cart piled high with bananas. When we crest the mountain, we stop where the air is cool. There's nothing left in our stomachs. The driver goes off in the bushes to pee, and Daddy climbs a rocky ledge. He waves his arms, motioning us to join him.

Berta clambers up the boulder, and Mama holds me until Daddy can grab me and pull me up beside him. He puts his arm around Mama and gives her a smacking kiss right on the lips. "There it is," he points. "Our new home."

The hillsides spill all the way down to the bluest water I've ever seen, a bay of shimmering light so bright it makes me blink. Daddy smiles. "See—there's Miches town." He gestures toward the inner curve of the bay to a scattering of small buildings crouched along a rocky shoreline with a few streets spreading out like a broken spider web. I blink and imagine the little houses are insects trapped in the web and then I shudder and tell myself not to think like that. I squint again at a long snaky river at the edge of town and then, to the right of it, a long sweep of sandy beach that stretches out like a sliver of new moon. The beach sweeps out to a point of land and disappears on the other side in a white-gold haze. The shore is lined with green fringe, and a smaller patch of a light color stands out like a ragged square of carpet. Daddy waves his arm toward the pale green at the far end of the bay. "There," he says as tears roll down his face. "That's Cocoloco Plantation. We'll always be able to pick it out from here."

"How come?" Berta asks.

"Because my plantings are young palms—all the other plantations have been here for decades and the fronds get dark green with age. So Cocoloco will always stand out."

"Always?"

"Well, until the trees grow really, really old—thirty or more years."

The driver peers over the rocks to see what we're all looking at. He smiles and I can see he's missing most of his front teeth. "*Bonito, sí.*" He nods. Pretty. Daddy lets me go and jumps back to the road.

I'm left alone up on the rock and it's dizzying way up here. This island is all I've known. We've moved several times before, but this is going to be, as Mama says, permanent. Forever, whatever that means. I'm lightheaded, and I whimper when I look down the edge of the cliff. Daddy glares at me as if I shouldn't be afraid and pulls me down to the ground without a word. I remember him telling Mama that if I were a boy I'd learn more quickly, and I figure he thinks I should just be able to jump down off the rock like it's nothing. We pack ourselves back into the car and the bay gets closer as we shudder downward.

We pull into the village of Miches, passing a church and small plaza. In a few minutes we're through what there is of town and the jeep sputters to a stop next to a pasture. A bunch of cows amble up to a sagging barbed wire fence, swishing their tails. Beyond the field is a wide stretch of brown water, the Yeguada River. Daddy has bought a small lot at the edge of town by a pasture, far away from the nearest house. The property fronts the bay and is bordered on one side by a *laguna* that used to drain out to the ocean but is now sealed up into a pond that keeps stray animals from entering our yard.

The village is mostly farmers, fishermen, and tradespeople.

The public *guagua* bus rattles its way over the mountain three times a week. It weaves through town, picking up passengers, passing the butcher shop over by the river, the tiny post office, the police station with its two officers and a three-legged dog, a *clínica* with a part-time doctor, and two grocery stores.

Instead of a nice concrete home with tile floors and rooms for servants—like other plantation owners in bigger towns build—our home will be small, with no servants, and it will be made entirely of aluminum. A neighbor sniffs and rolls his eyes. "*Aluminio?*" Daddy assures the doubters it will be as solid as concrete, and hurricane-proof.

While we wait for the house sections to arrive, we rent a cottage owned by someone from the capital who only visits Miches a few times a year. Don Elpidio, a local farmer we meet soon after moving in, whispers to Daddy over rum one night that the owners are *mala gente*, bad people. He makes a gesture with his hand, mimicking a slash across his throat. Daddy laughs. Mama is busy talking to his wife, Doña Selenia, and doesn't seem to hear the men's conversation. Berta is playing cards with their daughter Carmen, and they giggle as Berta tries to explain the rules of "Fish." I shift closer to Berta and beg her to let me play.

Berta waves me off at first. "You're too little."

"I'm not."

"*Déjala jugar,*" Carmen says. Let her play. Berta rolls her eyes but gives me some cards. I stick my tongue out at her. Then we both laugh and I forget about the bad people who own this house. The next morning I overhear Daddy repeating what Don Elpidio had said the night before—that our rented house belongs to two brothers who work for *El Jefe*, Trujillo himself. The dictator's full title is His Excellency Generalísimo Doctor

Rafael Leonidas Trujillo, Benefactor of the Republic, and he's ruled the Dominican Republic for twenty years. It's also okay to refer to him as *El Jefe*, The Chief. Mama and Daddy sit Berta and me down to tell us we are never, ever to speak badly about Trujillo or say anything at all about the government. But Don Elpidio says that the brothers who own our rented house are *asesinos*.

"I'm scared," I whisper to Mama that night when she tucks me into bed.

"There's nothing to be scared of."

"But Berta says *asesino* means killer. Will they hurt us?"

"No, no." Mama pats me on the head. "People like to talk about things they don't understand. These men are more like special police, and I'm sure they don't kill innocent people." She pulls the mosquito netting closed. "Go to sleep now. Everything's fine." Berta, in her bunk, snorts under her breath as if she doesn't believe Mama. I pull the web of netting around me and stare through my cocoon at the moonlight outside the window.

A TRUCK ARRIVES, bearing the metal sections that will become a house. The concrete foundation has already been laid. Sure enough, like Daddy promised, everything is aluminum—the posts, the roof, the walls, the windows, and the front and back doors. Daddy slices open one of the large cartons, pulling out one of several heavy sacks of fasteners. "See? Just like they said —five thousand nuts and bolts. That's it—all we need to put this whole goddamn thing together."

Within six days, we have a home—four small rooms with open passageways between them. The living room has a small dining table pushed against one wall. Mama rolls out the Peruvian rug made from llama wool that she's had since the year my parents got married and spent two years in the Andes Mountain on a job site. Daddy builds all our furniture and paints everything the same shade of turquoise. Everything. Bed frames, chairs, table, dressers, mirror frames, and even a shelf in the bathroom. His chair, in Adirondack style with wide arms, takes up an entire corner of the living room, and we kids are not to sit in it.

The front porch is a concrete extension designed like a half moon, the *media luna*. For parties and dancing, Daddy says. One night, after the house is finished, Daddy and Mama crank up our wind-up Victrola record player. Lantern glow and the light of a full moon overhead make everything feel almost cozy.

"See?" Daddy crows. "This is the life." He twirls Mama around to "When You're Smiling," a Perry Como song. He dips her back like the dancers on the cover of a tango record and points up at the moon. "All those working stiffs back in the States with their god-awful jobs and their boring lives—they don't know what they're missing."

He starts to sing, in Spanish, the song he made up about Miches. "*Ay, Miches, ay Miches, que linda es la vida aqui.*" How pretty life is in Miches. Mama laughs and finishes her drink.

Berta and I rattle dishes in the kitchen, soaping and rinsing, washing away the rum that clings to the glasses. Most nights are not like this. Daddy is drinking more and more until his voice gets slurry and he yells at us before slumping off to bed. I'm beginning to dread the nighttime.

Mama plants zinnias and ferns in a neat border alongside the kitchen. The finishing touch is the porch step, which Daddy says we'll build ourselves. Berta mixes the cement, and Mama and Daddy pour it into the wooden mold. When it's almost dry, Berta and I leave our footprints in the hardening concrete.

Mama takes her little finger and carves her and Daddy's initials into a corner. Mama decides to call our house "Casalata" because when it's all closed up it looks just like a tin can, or *lata*.

We have our first foreign visitors, members of the English consulate in Ciudad Trujillo, when they somehow hear about the Americans in this part of the island and find us. They've never seen a house like this. Daddy is dressed for company, in clean khaki shorts and a short-sleeved shirt. Usually he doesn't bother wearing shirts at all, and he is brown from working outdoors. He raps on the metal wall. "It's hurricane-proof. The locals here thought I was crazy when I told them what I was doing. I had a case of rum riding on this. With the road from El Seybo still mostly a donkey trail, no one could figure out how anyone could get a whole house over the mountain; they didn't know about prefab. Needless to say, I won the bet here—the *Micheros* toasted us with a roast pig and a guitar concert by one of the best damn musicians I've ever heard."

Mama is tall with crinkly blue eyes and soft brown hair with hints of gray. She has pinned her hair up and is wearing lipstick in honor of the guests. Her plaid shirt matches Daddy's. She sends Berta to the kitchen to refill the plate of Saltine crackers and cheese our guests have emptied. I sit at the edge of the porch, playing jacks and listening to the chatter, when I hear one of the visitors remark how well behaved we children are.

"Well, with all our travels, they have to be," my father says, leaning forward and lowering his voice. "We can take them anywhere. Hell, when I finished the London job there was a celebration at the Hotel Ritz—and the maître d' said he couldn't let us in because of the kids. I told him he wouldn't hear a squawk out of them. Right, Emily?"

My mother nods, but she also shakes her head in my

direction, like she's trying to tell Daddy something. I wonder what she's trying to say, but Daddy doesn't see her gesture. He swigs a glass of rum like it's water, then slides his glass over to Mama for another one.

I bounce the hard rubber ball and pick up a jack as a faint memory, a little fuzzy around the edges, comes into focus. It's a rainy day in a noisy big city—London—and the whole family is dressed up and eating lunch. I stare in wonder at what looks like a sky full of gold stars all bunched together and hanging down from a very high place, the stars bursting out of sparkling branches. A chandelier, Mama calls it.

I squash an ant that's climbing up on one of the jacks.

"So what's your secret?" our visitor asks Mama, swatting at a fly. Mama opens her mouth but Daddy answers.

"Oh, it's no secret, really. See, children—they're like horses. You just have to break their spirit when they're young. Then they don't give you any trouble." Daddy lights a cigarette, taking a long drag. He slurps some more rum then takes the guest by his arm and says, "Here, I'll show you the view from our dock. Prettiest harbor you ever saw."

Mama looks down and doesn't say anything. Berta stands in the doorway, frowning. She tugs at a strand of hair so hard she pulls it out. My stomach hurts, like the time the jeep that brought us over the mountain hit a deep gully where the road was all washed out. I don't really understand the business about horses, or what a spirit is—maybe a ghost?

That night I dream about broken bones that won't grow back right, ever. I wake crying from the nightmare, and Berta holds me, saying, "Shhh, you just had a bad dream."

I am afraid to move, in case I can't, but my arms and legs seem to work just fine.

Chapter Two

※

Tropical Storms

On mornings like this, after a rare night that Daddy hasn't yelled at us, Mama talks with a smile in her voice. Sleep softens Daddy's edges, like when I take my finger and blur the charcoal line on a drawing. A lopsided grin changes his face as he plays with me. I look like Daddy, lanky, with his brown eyes that droop just a bit at the ends, and my smile is wide like his too. Daddy likes to paint watercolors, and when I show an interest in art, he sends for a paint-by-number set from a store in the capital. He shows me how just the right amount of blue and yellow becomes the perfect green of a coconut frond.

I fetch the mail every day—the daily newspaper and the

few letters that find their way to us from Mama's sister, Aunt Betty. Mama sits on the porch in the morning with a cup of coffee and a cigarette, mending a torn shirt or making a new set of napkins. Her stitches are tiny, almost as straight as if she'd taken her work to the village seamstress with the foot-pedal Singer machine. Sometimes when Daddy is away by himself at the *finca*, she writes long letters to her sister. Some of the village ladies come to visit Mama in the afternoons. She serves them lemonade and cookies, but their visits aren't very long because Mama's not much for gossip. This irritates Doña Titina, who is always full of rumors or scandalous news, such as when a neighbor took a machete to her husband when she caught him with another woman or when the town drunk fell into the ocean and almost drowned. She says it like it was funny but it makes me shiver.

Daddy tinkers with his crafts in the backyard workshop, shaded by a giant *ceiba* tree. At a wooden workbench under a window he makes jewelry using shells and seeds. Berta and I scavenge the beach, piling rose cockles and coquinas here, green limpets and spider shells there. One of the trees in our yard grows a circular pod packed with boomerang-shaped seeds all held together in a big ball until it's ready to pop. On hot days, after ripening, a series of these explode and the pods spin out, two-toned brown and black. Daddy polishes them up until they shine like ebony. The wires strung across the window sag with jewelry. I stand on my tiptoes and look up at the parade of dangling earrings that sway like little dancers in the breeze. He ships most of his creations to the gift shops of fancy hotels in Ciudad Trujillo.

In a dark corner of the shop an oil portrait of Berta and me is tacked up inside a cabinet. It was painted when I was three and we lived in Spain for a year. Berta looks out from the canvas from pale blue eyes like she's not seeing anything at all. I stare, leaning forward, my eyes bright. Mama says we squirmed a lot during the sittings. My parents don't think the artist did a very good job, so they don't hang the painting in the house. Instead, it's pinned on the cabinet door like a dead butterfly, hidden away and forgotten. I think it's beautiful—we have bows in our hair and collared dresses, nothing like the khaki shorts and faded shirts we wear now.

Berta and I are schooled at home. Daddy builds an *enramada* in the back yard—a circle of cement with a center pole holding up a thatched roof. It's shaded by the cacao trees full of hard pods as big as papayas that we harvest to make chocolate. This is where we do our lessons. A big carton arrives from The Calvert School of Maryland with our school supplies for the year—new books, rulers, lined paper, lesson plans, yellow pencils, and pink rubber erasers. I'm in Grade One, and Berta is doing Grade Five. Every day Mama gives me my assignments, but Berta's old enough to read the lesson plans by herself, so she doesn't need Mama's help.

After Berta and I are finished with our daily schoolwork, Mama teaches me how to make cookies and breads from her 1951 *Joy of Cooking* cookbook. We have to improvise when the ingredients, like walnuts or pecans for nut bars, can't be found at the store. Yeasty, warm smells fill the house when we bake. Berta grinds the coffee beans and Mama shoves hunks of meat through another grinder. Sometimes she hums as she cooks. The sound calms my stomach and even Berta shows a smile or two. She never says so, but Mama seems happiest when it's just the three of us together, bumping into each other in the tiny kitchen, and Daddy is spending the night up at the *finca* tending to a harvest. We know the night ahead will be quiet and peaceful—no need to clench my stomach when six o'clock, Daddy's cocktail hour, comes with the threat of rum-talk, or—worse—hours of his drunken rantings before we can go to bed.

Daddy builds two boats from Chris Craft patterns he's brought from the States. The big one is an open skiff and will transport us across the bay to Cocoloco in good weather. The small rowboat, which we name *Frisky*, is for the *laguna*. In late September, a tropical storm sneaks up on us, different than the usual *chubascos*, the sudden rainstorms that file through, dumping rain as loud as thunder then moving on just as quickly. We wake up to the sound of crashing waves instead of the usual *lap-lap* rhythm. The white-capped sea has turned cloudy like beach glass and our skiff bucks at its line at the end of the new pier. Daddy hops into it and pulls up the anchor, surfing ashore. He steers the boat onto the rocky beach and ties it to the big avocado tree, which is swaying back and forth as if it doesn't know which way to go. He points to *Frisky*, bobbing in the *laguna*, and yells at us to bring it ashore too.

The weather is making me all jumpy and excited, and I close my arithmetic book and hold the line as Berta pulls *Frisky* ashore. After we've finished, I try to get back to my lesson. Instead I just draw lines with squiggly tops that are supposed to be coconut trees all bent over from wind. I add figures of a woman and two children running away from the edge of the sea. I make their pictures larger than the trees behind them, just like Daddy taught me. He calls it "foreshortening"; he says it makes the picture look real.

In the house, the battery-operated Zenith radio is tuned to weather news. Daddy scribbles the latitude and longitude of the storm, now a hurricane called Charlie and just a few miles from the south coast of the island. At sunset, the sky shrieks orange and purple. The waves pound our pier and loosen its planks. We stand at the edge as the waves churn, and, afraid I'll blow away, I cling to Berta, who says I'm being a silly goose.

The sky darkens into blue-black. Back inside Casalata, the kerosene lanterns flicker and the aluminum walls glow bright then dim. Daddy says we have to keep the windows open so the air pressure stays even, but then the rains come and we close everything up. After dinner we play Monopoly in silence because the rain and the wind drown out our voices. They even drown out Daddy.

By morning the overflowing river pours into the *laguna*, which has broken through to the ocean, washing away two young trees. Mama kneels by the hole where the saplings once grew and clucks her tongue. "They never had a chance to take hold. If they'd been older, the roots would have kept them from being torn out of the ground." She sighs, a long broken sound. "Oh, well," she finally says, "We'll just plant something else here —we don't even have to dig a new hole, so that will be easy."

We pile up the fallen leaves and palm fronds. Our pier is destroyed. For days afterward, local boys scour the beach for missing planks and sell them back to Daddy for a few pesos. In the meantime, the shattered pilings stick out of the water like broken nubs of teeth, brown and jagged. The waters recede and the sandbar heals like scar tissue, sealing the *laguna* once again into its own world. I explore the changes brought by the storm, spending hours suspended in the rowboat, drifting, looking at the water below the surface. It darkens to a ruby red, still clear enough to see snapping turtles and small fish and pollywogs.

Below that is a layer of silt that looks like dark chocolate, which I disturb with a stick and watch settle. I'm scared of the unseen bottom—the quicksand that I'm afraid will trap and suck me down if I fall in. It doesn't matter that I can swim; the fear is always there below the surface.

I get the same feeling when I pedal my bicycle past the empty house we used to rent, the one owned by Trujillo's *asesinos*, or when it's nighttime and Daddy is yelling at Mama or us—something he's started to do more and more. His drunken jags are like a never-ending series of storms. We get very good at predicting the weather ahead. His eyes are like a barometer, telling me if it's just a light squall passing through or the beginning of a cyclone that will pound us through the night. Part of me wishes that Charlie could have been a monster storm, something that would make everything in our life change—something that would jolt Daddy into being different. I don't know yet about the storm that will shatter our family into pieces of wreckage, like our broken pier.

Chapter Three

※

Friends and Enemy

A year after we move to Miches, one of Daddy's workers
brings us a puppy, a wiggly ball of white fur and pink
tongue. "*Para las niñas,*" he says. For the girls. Daddy first says
no, but Mama begs him and he finally says we can keep him.
The dog likes to bob about in the *laguna*, chasing the loons that
are too smart to let him come anywhere near, so Berta names
him Bobby. My job is to groom him; that's a fancy word for
pulling off ticks. Every afternoon, I sit him down on the porch
step with a pair of tweezers and a jar of kerosene. I find the ticks
that are all filled up with blood, as fat as little grapes. Bobby
usually sleeps outside, in the *enramada*. His favorite spot is
under Daddy's chair, except when he's drunk. Then Bobby's tail

curls under and he slinks under my bed. I sneak him up to my bunk and he licks my face.

Berta and I have made good friends in Miches, and we play together after their school lets out and our own lessons are over. Daddy doesn't think much of the local schools. He says Trujillo promises every child an education, but it's all propaganda and they only learn what *El Jefe* wants them to believe. "I'll bet there isn't a single adult in this village who could pick out North America or Africa or anyplace on a map besides this island and maybe Cuba or Puerto Rico," he says.

On Fridays it's my turn to go grocery shopping and I haul out my bicycle and set out, stopping first at a stall where I can find the local delicacy, *dulce de coco*. María la Sorda has a candy stand in front of her house, and she boils up batches in a big cauldron. Bobby and I follow the smell of the charcoal fire and a strong sweet aroma on her street.

"*Buenos días*," I say too loudly. She opens her mouth in a toothless grin and her gray hair shakes in its bun. She grates coconut meat into cheesecloth and squeezes a stream of the white liquid into a simmering stew of milk and sugar. As the candy thickens, she tosses in a bunch of twigs tied into a small bundle, and the air fills with the bite of cinnamon and the scent of vanilla beans. After pulling the heavy cauldron off the fire, she ladles a layer of *dulce* onto a large sheet where it hardens before she cuts it into squares for sale. I buy ten pieces to take home. María la Sorda gives me a coconut embrace that feels warm and smoky and good and makes me wish Mama would hug me like that sometimes. I just wish she'd hug me, period. With my still-warm candy in hand, I race to the grocery store with Mama's list and hope I don't run into my enemy, who often lies in wait for me at Juan Kair's market. I careen past scolding chickens, avoiding most potholes along the gravel street. Bobby trots alongside, barking at roosters. Since there are only a few jalopies, the bus, and a few battered trucks in the entire village, I'm not worried about traffic, but I am on alert for my one enemy—a boy named King Kong.

Once I arrive at the store, I scan the surroundings before dropping the bike in a corner just outside the old wooden building. Maybe today I'll be safe. I step inside the store, which smells of green coffee and sweet oranges. Bobby follows me, sniffing and wagging his tail. Señor Kair wraps a purchase in brown paper. He has a kind face and white hair that rises in tufts. He reaches out for Mama's list and pulls a worn pencil out from behind his ear. I want him to hurry, but he takes his time assembling the goods. Rice, red beans, sugar, and a chunk of beef, all carefully weighed on the rusty scale. I love the smells, even the stink of raw meat as it leaks red through the paper. He ticks off the rest of the list: A bottle of rum, of course. Coconut oil, soap, and a loaf of *pan de agua*, the local bread. He finally hands the heavy bag down to me and gives Bobby a treat, a stale bun he gulps down happily. I'm ready to load up the basket and wheel away home. I know that once I lock the backyard gate behind me, I'll be safe.

But no luck today. King Kong grabs my bike just as I come outside with my hands full of groceries. My bicycle disappears around the corner before I can grab it. With a nasty laugh, he pedals out of sight, his shirt flapping like a brown moth. He's the local troublemaker. I know he'll just ride around for several minutes before getting bored and dropping the bicycle a few blocks away. He just does it to scare me, since everyone in town knows it's mine. Today, Jesús the barber pedals back with it ten minutes after it has disappeared. I'm sitting on the curb, trying not to cry. Bobby licks my face and whimpers. When I get home, I tell Mama what happened, but she says she can't do anything; besides, I got the bike back. That night I pull Bobby up into my bed with me and he settles in by my toes. I tell him he did a good job trying to protect me from the bad boy. He licks my fingers and snorts, and it makes me smile.

King Kong got his nickname from the occasional traveling picture show that turns up a couple of times a year. This caravan sets up a generator in the *gallera*, the village cockfighting arena down by the river, and they tack up movie posters all over town, promising danger and excitement. On a Saturday evening just after sunset, children and adults flock into the thatch-roofed shack. For ten *centavos* everyone sits on hard wooden bleachers in the darkened shed, which smells like chicken droppings and dust. We huddle as black-and-white images jerk across the screen, which is really just a white sheet stretched between two poles. The movies are dubbed in Spanish. Cowboy Westerns with snorting horses and gun-shooting heroes are popular. Other times we get cliffhangers with villains, or stories about monstrous dragons.

One night a young boy jumps in front of the screen, his shadow looming huge, and startles the audience. The movie is about a big ape that climbs tiny skyscrapers, holding a wriggling girl in his huge hand. Imitating the onscreen action, the boy hops and pounds his chest, yelling *"Yo soy King Kong!"*—I am King Kong!—before someone shoos him outside.

The name sticks. On the days when I'm lucky and Señor Kair himself chases the boy away before he can nab my bike, I'm still afraid. King Kong just lopes off, unrepentant, taunting, *"La próxima vez, la próxima vez"*—next time, next time, I'll get you.

Chapter Four

❄

Rum

Daddy isn't a drunk. He isn't one because drunks—he says
—start drinking in the morning. In the daytime Daddy
is hard at work with *finca* business. At lunchtime he makes
Mama laugh with corny jokes, or tells her how good her
macaroni casserole tastes. After siesta he shows Berta how to
change the tire on the bicycle, or teaches me more about
perspective so I can draw trees and people with everything in
the right proportion. While the sun is shining, I'm not afraid of
him. It's like when the tide is out and the beach is clean and
shiny with shells and treasures to be found. He doesn't drink
until evening, and he says it's only to relax, but that's not true.
He starts with tall glasses of rum and Coca-Cola at sunset to
wind down, but that's really when he begins to wind *up*. His

drinking is like a storm tide that comes in and washes over everything and turns Daddy into something scary.

Berta and I dread the dusk. We never know whether it's going to be a good night or a bad one. Mama drinks, too. She's happy if Daddy's in a good mood, or silent and sad looking if he's not. On a good night they'll play Scrabble on the porch while supper is cooking, laughing and smoking *cigarillos*, the unfiltered cigarettes that smell both sweet and rotten at the same time. Sometimes Berta and I play games with them too—Scrabble, Monopoly, or Parcheesi. Then we have supper, clean up the dishes, and settle into reading by lamplight until it's time for bed.

But on bad nights, Daddy keeps drinking until he's wobbly and sloppy, and anything can happen. He might decide we'll all go dancing at the local bar, but when we get there he falls down drunk on the dance floor and Mama and Berta have to prop him between them to walk home. Or he'll invite whoever is in the bar to come to our house for a fiesta, and then change his mind as people start to arrive. On those nights Berta or I have to meet our guests at the gate and say we're sorry, but Daddy's not feeling well after all, so there will be no party. Or he'll get all wound up about something he reads in the news and the whole family has to sit in the living room as he rants and raves about whatever is bothering him. Mama doesn't interfere; she smokes one cigarette after another and hunches in a corner seat, almost as if she's a ghost. Sometimes she cries.

Even good nights can turn awful, because when they have parties, Daddy makes Berta and me put on the grass skirts and paper leis he brought from Hawaii the year he repaired ships' electrical systems in Pearl Harbor after the war and we have to dance the hula in front of guests. Berta said no to that activity, just once, and was spanked. I squirm with embarrassment and try to move my arms like Daddy showed us real hula dancers do. I don't want to be spanked. Even on good nights, Berta chews on her fingernails and I get stomachaches.

When I run away for the first time, sticks and gravel poke sharply against my skin and waves rake against the stony shore behind me with a dull hiss. I'm crouched just beyond the front gate. My stomach hurts, my head is tight. At this time of night there's no one else on the dirt path that skirts the shore. I hear my name being called. I lie still, barely breathing, afraid to be found, afraid not to be found. I don't even know how I got here, and I'm too scared to go any farther in the darkness.

Daddy is very drunk; he's been screaming at Mama. I don't remember exactly what he said. He swung around to slap at her face, but his hand missed and he stumbled. She cringed like a dog that just got kicked, and her hands trembled. She wrung them together as if she could wash away his words. My head filled up with the sound and it was too loud; it was all noise. He leaned forward and I was afraid he'd hit her this time, but he knocked over a glass instead. He stood there, weaving, looking at his spilled drink, saying, "Goddamn, goddamn, GODDAMN."

I know that no matter what happens, Berta and I have to stay put until Daddy says we can go to bed. I wanted to pee so badly I was wetting myself, but I held it in until finally I whimpered "I have to go" and just got up. Nobody moved. I ran to the bathroom, shaking, and when I was done, I couldn't go back to the yelling room. Then I was outside by the kitchen door and I don't remember running at all, but here I am, looking through the hibiscus along the fence line toward the flickering lamplight inside Casalata.

I'm here, I'm here, I cry in my head. "Stop yelling at Mama,"

I whisper as if Daddy can hear me. My throat aches; it's worse than when I have a cold. I shudder as I huddle against cold rocks and sticker vines.

Flashlights poke through the darkness like fireflies. A light finds me; it's Berta. She's shaking, even though it's not cold. She pulls me up easily. "Where did you think you were going?" she asks quietly, not scolding.

"I don't know."

"You scared them. Me too." Berta reaches for me.

"I don't care." I start wailing again until I lose my breath.

Berta holds on to my arm as if I'll try to escape. As if there's anywhere else to go.

"I hate him," I whisper, the words barely making a sound.

"Yeah." Her voice is flat.

"He's going to spank me."

"I know. Mama says he didn't used to be like this; it's just the rum talking." She holds me against her and I can feel her heart beat. She's afraid too, I can smell it.

More flashlights. Mama's white face looms out of the shadows. Bobby barks and wags his tail as if we're playing a game. Daddy looks at me, but for once doesn't say anything. When we get inside the house, instead of spanking me, Daddy goes to bed without another word. So it's Mama who turns me over her knee. When Daddy hits me, it really hurts, but Mama's slaps are softer, like she doesn't actually mean it. She shakes each time her hand hits my bottom as if it hurts her too.

Afterwards, Berta lets me curl up beside her in bed and whispers into my hair. "When we're older, we can live together, and I'll take care of you."

I think of Mama all alone with Daddy and gulp, "What about Mama?"

"Oh, we'll be grown up by then. It'll just be you and me. Now go to sleep and don't kick me."

I decide to pray, but I can't figure out who or what God is. All I know about God is he's supposed to be an old bearded man in a white cape. I don't really want to pray to poor Jesus. I've seen pictures of him hanging in the grocer's store—nailed up and bleeding from the cross, looking skinnier than Daddy, even. Daddy says God doesn't exist. I shut my eyes as I listen to Berta's sleeping noises and talk in my head to anybody who will maybe, someday, listen and make things better, like in the stories I read with happily-ever-after endings.

DADDY ⤴

Chapter Five

❄

Cocoloco

Daddy says coconuts are just like him: they don't survive in cold climates—they must have warm, sandy soil and plenty of sunshine. They grow between the Tropics of Cancer and Capricorn. Cocoloco is right in the zone at latitude 18° N. In the daytime, when Daddy is sober, he sometimes reads to me from the article he's writing for *National Geographic* about our *finca*.

He says he hopes the magazine will publish it. He writes in longhand, and then Mama types it up on the Royal portable. His article is how I know so much about coconuts, which originated in southern Asia. Because the nuts float, they bobbed across the Pacific Ocean to far shores, carried by currents until they made landfall and sprouted to new life throughout the tropics. The survivors of these voyages dot the water's edge all along Cocoloco's shoreline. The raggedy palms, starved of real soil, still manage to put down roots on the beach just above the high water mark. The roots are shallow and spreading and hold tight to the earth like hundreds of tentacles.

Coconut palms rarely snap. After a hurricane's punch, they'll recover and just keep growing, bent and gnarled. Twisted almost sideways by storms, they stretch out over the shallows then finally bend upward toward the sun. The green crowns cast spidery shadows on the water below. I like to climb these castaways because I can sprawl out on the nearly horizontal trunk. Hugging the warm, rough surface, I lean over and watch the waves break just a few feet below me while I'm held safely in my swaying perch.

Daddy's drinking gets worse, but our palms grow straight up and proud, and they produce more and more coconuts each harvest. In a few more years we'll be in full production, unless a hurricane hits. He says once the trees are strongly rooted, we won't have to worry about storms at all. Maybe, I think, my family is like a bunch of coconuts washed onto the beach, trying to spread our own roots into new earth. At night I sometimes have nightmares of a wall of water coming ashore. I have to find something solid to hang on to, and I run toward a palm tree, but I can never get my arms completely around the trunk, and I wake up just before I'm carried off into the ocean.

At Cocoloco, we're growing three varieties of palms, and they can pollinate themselves, but according to Daddy, bees and hornets help the process, and plenty of those buzz around everywhere. Copra is the dried meat of the coconut that Daddy sells to companies that turn it into soap and cooking oil. Daddy says that in India, where he first got the idea for Cocoloco, they call coconut palms "trees of heaven" because every single part can be used. In Miches, layers of coconut fronds become roofs for houses, or are braided into baskets and chair seats, and trunks are split into logs. Daddy uses the hard inner shell as fuel to dry the coconut crops into copra. In his workshop he makes lampshades from the fiber of husks, and he turns the half-shells into pretty bowls. Mama cooks with coconut oil and we all wash our hair and dishes with coconut soap. We drink the tangy water of the young green nuts, and eat the jelly inside like custard. When the nutmeat is mature it hardens to a texture like raw carrot, which Mama grates into filling for coconut cream pies and frosting for cakes.

Daddy says coconuts only have one enemy besides hurricanes: the rhinoceros beetle. He writes about it for his story:

Most diseases that occur in the palms are caused by either extreme dry or wet weather, and we have had very minor losses. Since the palms don't put out a taproot, but hundreds of roots about the diameter of a pencil, spreading in all directions, we planted them thirty-four feet apart, which allows plenty of room. As the fronds from one palm seldom reach those of another, the possibility of disease spread is also lessened. The biggest danger to the palms was during the first four years of growth, caused by the "catarones" or rhinoceros beetles. They burrow into the trunk near the ground, eat out the heart and the palm dies. We tried various methods of control and ended up by merely digging them out carefully and killing them. The men who hunted them also hacked into rotting logs to find hatching places and destroy the larvae. Since the beetles seldom attack a mature palm, this danger is practically over.

I'VE SEEN THOSE DISEASED PALMS, pockmarked with ugly holes; the fronds hanging limp, dying. Once Berta said Daddy uses alcohol to try to kill whatever is eating him alive. It makes me think of the rhinoceros beetles, crawling around inside him, making him sick, but it's the rum that's doing all the damage to Daddy, as far as I can figure. She says Daddy has bad thoughts inside, and that rum helps him forget them. "What kind of bad thoughts?" I ask. Berta says she doesn't know what they are either, and looks away, picking at her lip, like she knows something she can't say.

Reading Daddy's article about our *finca*, you'd never know that anything is ever wrong here. No bad thoughts or memories or drunkenness—life is just wonderful. He never says much about us in his story—it's all about coconuts.

As coco palms bear a new bunch monthly which ripens in a year's time, and can be harvested every three months, the plantation is also divided into three parts. Thus the first week of every month is used in harvest and the second in husking. The shell-chipping and drying start during the second or third week, depending on the quantity, and this is repeated in the next area in the following month. Maintenance of the land and palms is done by other men who work steadily with the versatile machete, cleaning the debris from around the palms and cutting down the underbrush which grows thick and fast here in the tropics.

DADDY MAKES IT SOUND LIKE the whole cycle of harvest is orderly and everything happens like clockwork. He's in charge of the copra drying, and we make the trip to Cocoloco from Miches every few days during each harvest. If the ocean is too rough to have the boat in the water, we journey by foot to the *finca*, taking twice as long. Crossing the Yeguada River might be

easy at low tide, or a scary trip through stiff current at high tide
as we balance food sacks above our heads and hope we won't
slip on a submerged branch or rock. From the other side of the
river, it's four kilometers to Cocoloco. From the time I hoist my canvas bag over my shoulder, I'm
full of dread. We'll be spending three days up at Cocoloco on
this trip, so we're laden with knapsacks full of groceries and
books. If it were low tide, the walk on the beach would be a
stroll on smooth ground. But it's high tide. The sand is soft and
sticky, and we sink up to our ankles in mushy wetness. The
Jovero River lies just before the *finca*. Usually that river stays
shoaled up, puddling into a shallow pond, shaded by grape leaf
bushes and *almendra* trees, but today it has broken through its
banks, cutting a wide path to the bay. After a storm it's always
hard to gauge its depth, and I already know Berta or I will be, as
usual, the guinea pigs sent ahead to see how deep the water is.
With us smaller figures as measuring sticks, Daddy will
calculate the best crossing spot for the rest of the family, where
our food and supplies have a better chance of staying dry. It is
my turn at the Jovero.

Mama takes my pack and I step into the rushing water. I
grit my teeth and stumble ahead. Every step is torture because I
can't see below the surface and I'm frightened of what I might
step on. After a few yards, the bottom suddenly drops off and I
lose my footing. Swept away in the current, I stroke furiously
across to the other side, gasping and swallowing water. Daddy,
Mama and Berta then take a different route, wading into the
ocean where the breakers collide with the current, slowing its
rush. Berta carries Bobby, but he wiggles out of her arms and
swims easily across. Even though the water is almost waist high,
they keep their balance and the food stays dry. Wet and angry, I

spit out saltwater as Mama heaves the pack back onto my shoulders.

"You'll be dry by the time we get to the *finca*," Mama says. She lights a cigarette and pushes dripping hair out of my face. I twist my head away and glare at Daddy's back. He's already halfway to the path that leads to the house on stilts.

Daddy designed the *finca* house. The downstairs is open, a slab of concrete with a picnic table and bench. Our kitchen is a cabinet in the corner that holds a Coleman camp stove and lantern, and shelves with dishware and staples. A rain barrel perches in a corner, but we can't count on rain, so we also have a pump outside that gushes out brackish water. Upstairs, a small porch leads into a single room with two sets of bunk beds divided by a curtain. Mama and Daddy have one side, and Berta and I the other. The windows and door are screened to keep out tarantulas and centipedes.

It's very quiet at Cocoloco, and Daddy seems happiest here. He doesn't drink as much away from the village. But that thought doesn't comfort me. I shiver, not from cold, but from the leftover fright of the Jovero River. Berta primes the pump as Mama puts away our food, and I rinse off my sandy clothes. I wish I could run away, but there's nowhere to go. Besides, I already tried that once.

Chapter Six

※

Accidents and Mysteries

The summer has been quiet. We're not getting any news magazines, or the other US publications we subscribe to, so we're stuck with the local papers filled with stories celebrating *El Jefe's* twenty-fifth anniversary as the country's leader. One article points out that there have been no civil wars since his rule, a first for the nation. *Gracias a Dios y Trujillo*, of course. Thanks to God and Trujillo, always.

We get a letter from the Jonsens in Ciudad Trujillo. They're coming for a visit at the end of August. Other than the Breedens, who are American, they are my parents' closest friends. They have three children. Their son Jaak is nine, a year younger than me, and I have a crush on him even if I only see him once or twice a year. The Jonsens came to the island as refugees from Estonia when their country was overtaken by Germany in World War II. Daddy says Trujillo opened the doors to many Eastern Europeans fleeing Nazi persecution, and that *El Jefe* offered this asylum because he was trying to improve his reputation with the Allied nations. I don't understand about the reputation part, but Berta fills me in. Many years before we ever moved to the island, Trujillo had ideas of overthrowing Haiti, at one point ordering the killing of thousands of Haitians living on the Dominican side of the border between the two countries. According to Berta, this made the US government very mad. So Trujillo, to make the Americans overlook the Haitian mess, decided to publicize this gesture of goodwill—offering home and freedom to World War II victims. Berta says Trujillo's plan didn't really work out too well. The first batch of refugees was sent to the north, where they had to machete their way through brush and jungle to clear homesteads. A small colony became dairy farmers, and their descendants still live near Sosua. One of Carmen's uncles goes to that village, west of the Samana Peninsula, to buy their cheeses. He says many farmers there have blue eyes and *cabello amarillo*—yellow hair. Other refugees found their way to the capital and started businesses there.

I ask Daddy, if Trujillo did those other bad things, then why are we here?

Daddy waves his arms, as if impatient, and says, "Oh, that was a long time ago—you can't understand about politics, and besides, everything is stable now, and I wouldn't have brought the whole damn family here if it wasn't safe."

Berta says that Trujillo only wanted the foreigners for the money and skills they would bring and so the settlers would marry Dominicans and help "lighten" the race. She says Trujillo, who pretends to be of pure Spanish blood, has a Haitian grandmother, and that he powders his face and neck to look whiter than he really is.

The Jonsens arrive for a week stay. We only see the family once a year, but I've liked Jaak since I was five. He has sky-blue eyes and straight blond hair that flops into his face. He's the most handsome boy I've ever seen, and the only boy or girl my age I can talk to in English.

I'm so excited I kick Jaak in the shins as we take *Frisky* for a row around the *laguna* and he falls in the water. I don't mean to hurt him. He hauls himself up off the mud bank and I can see he's trying not to cry as he limps toward Casalata. Embarrassed, I yell "I'm sorry," but he's inside and doesn't hear me. I accidentally let go of the boat rope and it now bumps against the reeds on the opposite shore. I grit my teeth and swim out to bring it back. I'm afraid of the water, full of snapping turtles and dark secrets where it's deep and the bottom is hidden. On shore, Jaak is waiting for me, signaling me for me to throw the rope up to him. He's laughing at me as I slip in the mud and fall back in the water. I notice his left shin is bright red and scraped raw. I guess we're even.

"I'm sorry," I say again as bits of pond scum stick to my clothes and skin.

"You're crazy, you know?" he says. I just nod and keep my gaze on his outstretched arm, which is already getting strong, even at nine years old. Pale hairs cover his forearm like a soft mist. I've been reading *Lorna Doone*. I decide Jaak is John Ridd, Lorna's suitor, and he's pulling me out from the dangerous bog on the foggy moors of England, away from the quicksand that can swallow a person alive.

The night of the Jonsens' arrival, Mama and Daddy catch up on news they've brought from the capital. We kids are playing cards in corner of the porch when the adults' voices get low, always a signal that something important is being said. I perk up my ears to listen and Berta frowns slightly and also turns her head. Mr. Jonsen is talking about Jesus de Galindez, a professor at a New York university, who suddenly disappeared in a subway station after writing a paper that said bad things about Trujillo. Everyone is saying Trujillo had him kidnapped and brought to the Dominican Republic, and that he's been murdered by *El Jefe*'s orders. Daddy and Mama are leaning in, paying close attention.

I think back to when we rented the green house, before Casalata was built, and how scared and mad Daddy was when he found out that the owner was one of *El Jefe*'s hired killers. We've stayed clear of the owners since then when they come to spend time in their vacation cottage, except for when there were some young girls, nieces I guess, who arrived in the summer and wanted to play. They seemed normal to me, except for having new clothes in the latest fashions. But they weren't that friendly to my other Dominican friends, like somehow city girls were more important than daughters of seamstresses or grocers. They played with me because we owned a *finca*, or because we were Americans. I've already figured out being a *Norteamericana* makes me different no matter what. At least no one will want to hurt us.

Casalata fills with laughter during the rest of the Jonsens' visit and time passes too quickly. When our guests leave, stillness fills the air. I feel a sense of waiting, but I'm not sure why. No American news magazines arrive, just the stray *National Geographic* every few months. Early the next year, Mr.

Jonsen sends us a *Life* magazine with a story about Gerald Murphy, an American pilot who worked for the local Dominican airline. I remember reading an article about him in *El Caribe* newspaper a few months ago, about his empty car found by an ocean cliff, near Ciudad Trujillo. They said it probably was an accident. But the *Life* article gives me goose bumps because it connects the pilot to the professor, Galindez. The story says Murphy flew Galindez (dead or alive, it wasn't clear) to the Dominican Republic shortly after the professor vanished. Now Murphy has disappeared too, and this article says it's no accident—it's murder. The American government is investigating both cases.

Later in the week, after we've all read the magazine from cover to cover, I notice this particular story has been ripped out. Doing chores the next day, I find it in pieces in the kitchen garbage, under a wad of coffee grounds. Mama and Daddy don't say another word about it, but it's clear they don't want anyone else to know they've read the story about the missing professor and pilot.

Chapter Seven

✻

Church Bells and Cock Fights

Everybody in Miches goes to church on Sundays except us. The bells peal twice, loud and clear, once for the eight o'clock service and then again for ten o'clock mass. The sound ripples through town all the way to the river. Daddy is anti-Pope and very anti-Catholic, and doesn't much care for the Protestants either, although there aren't many of those in Miches. The priest, Padre Daniel, is the only other foreigner in town, a French Canadian who speaks Spanish with a heavy accent. He drops in one day soon after Casalata is put together to invite our family into the church fold.

Daddy and Mama welcome him and offer him coffee. The minute the Padre mentions the church and how he'd like us to join, Daddy tightens his jaw. Before he can speak, Mama opens her mouth and speaks in Spanish.

"I'm sorry, Padre. We're Protestant."

"The hell I am," Daddy says in English and stomps out of the house.

The priest shakes his head and takes Mama's hand in his. "I'll pray for you anyway."

Daddy turns his head, still in hearing distance. "We don't need your prayers."

Mama's face is red. Her hands rub each other, her knuckles tight knots. My face is hot too, and I stare at the ground in shame. I'm only seven, but I know better than to speak. Berta escapes by cutting around the corner of the house with some washing she's hanging up on the clothesline by the bougainvillea bush.

Mama finds words. "Thank you, Padre, for taking the time. I'm so sorry."

The priest lowers his voice. "It's all right. God bless you and your family. If you ever need anything, I'm at your service."

He nods and smiles at me, patting my cheek before walking slowly down the path. After he's gone, Daddy slams the gate closed and crunches back up the gravel path as if he's still sore. Mama raises her arm limply, as if asking permission to speak.

Daddy interrupts. "He's not setting foot in this house again, and don't you forget it. I don't trust those do-gooders." Daddy is just winding up now, and once again we get to hear how the world is going to end badly because of the Catholics. There won't be enough food for all of them until the goddamned church stops telling them to be fruitful and multiply.

When my friends learn we're not Catholic, Niña says she prays for my soul. Daisy says she is sorry that I'll be going to

hell when they will all, "*si Dios quiere*"—God willing—be in
heaven. I don't care about that, because heaven sounds like a
fairy tale and I know fairy tales are not true. The only time I feel
like I'm in church is when I visit Niña. The word *niña* just
means "girl," and the name stuck after her mother died and she
went to live with her grandmother. The other girls think she'll
become a nun. Her house is wooden and very small. In the tiny
living room a painting of Jesus bleeding on the cross hangs next
to the *Virgen de Altagracia* holding a baby Jesus. A portrait of
Trujillo hangs crooked on the opposite wall. A table is covered
with a tablecloth with lace borders that Niña stitched by hand.
Candles flicker in cloudy glasses next to a Bible and book of
prayers. A set of amber rosary beads glow in the candlelight. My
achy stomach calms down in Niña's house; there's no danger
here.

Whether it's because of religion or not, Daddy doesn't
usually drink on Sundays, so it's a day of rest for all of us. I lie
awake in the early morning watching the light breeze riffle the
mosquito netting above my head. The church bells add music,
and I'm safe in my mesh cocoon. I hear Daddy talking and
Mama making breakfast. It's Berta's turn to set the table. I
wiggle under the sheets to the twitter of birds in the orange
tree. On Sundays Mama lets Berta have a little coffee in her hot
milk, but I won't be allowed coffee until I'm older. Berta brings
her cup into the bedroom and gives me a sip. Making little eye
contact with Daddy, who gave us a three-hour sermon last night
on the evils of the church, I take my place at the table. He
coughs, says good morning, and attends to his food. I put on a
smile. The bells ring again—last call for the eight o'clock mass.

Even though Daddy has forbidden me to set foot inside the
church, I've peeked in as the stained glass light streams in,

turning everything red and gold. I've seen the statue of Jesus on his cross, blood dripping down from the holes where he's nailed to the wood, and the clay Virgin Mary holding him in her arms.

All my friends are in church now, sprinkling holy water, fingering their rosary beads, praying, or getting their sins absolved. I wish I were there, sitting on the hard wooden seat that smells of moldy wood and incense, getting my sins washed away. I have lots of bad thoughts. I know it's wrong to think how wonderful life would be if Daddy were out of our lives, but I dream of standing tall and yelling right back at him to *STOP yelling, drinking, and hurting us*. I never do that, of course— those are evil thoughts. It sure would be nice to be absolved of my terrible sins; like Daisy was the time she cursed after her brother knocked her into a mud puddle. "Padre Daniel said to do three hail Marys, and that was it—God forgave me."

Zuleica says Padre Daniel prays for our souls in church, but he never again tries to bring us into his fold. But even so, he manages to gain Daddy's respect. When Berta has a fever of 104 degrees for a whole week, it's Padre Daniel who drives her and Mama over the mountain in his jeep, hurrying, hurrying to the medical clinic in El Seybo, where they have antibiotics and doctors. He sits by my sister's bedside while she hallucinates with fever, and gets permission for Mama to stay with Berta, right in the same room, until it's safe to bring her home to Miches. And it's the Padre who knocks on our door with reports from the clinic, and whose housekeeper brings over a stew for Daddy and me, alone together in our house for days. Sundays remind me of Padre Daniel and his goodness, and while Daddy ignores the sound of the church bells, they hum inside me like a bright hope.

By noon, all the worshipers go home for the Sunday meal,

followed by siesta time until two o'clock. Miches is silent in the heat of midday, gathering in on itself, breathing for a while, sins washed away by the bright morning sun and God's love.

Another religion takes over in the afternoon. After siesta, men throughout the village begin their weekly pilgrimage for the afternoon service—not at the church this time. Men and boys flood steadily down San Antonio Street toward the *gallera*. I've bicycled by the village's cockfighting arena on days when no one is around and peeked through the warped slats. A few blocks away from our house, the circular structure is rimmed with five rows of crude benches. At the center is hard-packed ground, the ring where the roosters will fight. Mama says this is no place for us, so I don't tell her I've already explored the empty ring where the dirt smells bad and bloodied feathers lie scattered like leaves.

On Sundays, spectators crowd the battlefield and small boys hang from poles or any place they can get a good view after all the benches fill up. There are no women or girls in sight, except for Maria La Sorda, who sets up her candy cart outside. The siesta-time quiet gives way first to small waves of shouts, then the sound becomes a roar, punctuated by curses or yells of victory. The *gallera* is the afternoon worship, and the offerings to the gods are the fighting machines that two men hold in their arms down on the ground. These roosters have been trained for months, and the best of them fight on Sunday afternoons. In the Dominican version of fights at an ancient Roman coliseum, bets are placed, rum flows, and the battles are waged for hours. By mid-afternoon the roar of the *gallera* is amplified as hundreds of feet pound the benches in excitement or frustration. It becomes just noise after a while, like when there's a downpour and you can't hear a thing because it's so loud. As the sun begins to set, the thunder fades, and the winners and losers filter out and stumble home. They can repent their sins next Sunday morning in church.

I wonder what it's like to yell and root for a bird to kill another. I feel so sorry for the roosters. Days before a fight, grown men carry their *gallos* under their arms like you'd cradle a kitten, taking them everywhere, showing them off. The birds have shiny feathers, bright eyes, and sharp spurs. Afterwards, the ones who live through a day at the fights are all tattered, and they're left in their coops to heal while a fresh young bird is groomed for the next fight.

If I wasn't forbidden to go into the church, I'd be praying there every Sunday morning for the poor roosters. Instead, I read my book and try to ignore the sour taste in my mouth when the noise from the *gallera* grows into a roar—the sound of victory and the sound of death.

Chapter Eight

※

Light and Noise

One of my jobs is to trim the wick on the kerosene lanterns, our only source of light the first few years in Miches. I also have to pick out the insects that fall in, attracted to the light, burned by the flame. When I try to rescue them I end up burning myself too so I watch them flutter and crumble to ash. I also have to wash the lantern chimneys when one of us has turned the wick up too high for better light, causing the glass to get all smoky and dark.

Light also attracts crickets; their high-pitched buzz reverberates through Casalata's aluminum walls, causing Daddy to scream at one of us to take the Flit gun and find and kill them. Since all we want is for Daddy to not get mad at us at night, Berta and I become adept at hunting down these night creatures and annihilating them with the poison spray from the gun. Our mostly green lawn is pockmarked with yellowing grass, battlegrounds where we've won or lost the wars against the invaders. Other than the crickets, nights in Miches (except for Daddy's ranting) are quiet.

The only exception is in June, when an ancient drumming ceremony called a *velorio* takes place over nine nights, just before the celebration of the town's patron saint. It's always a surprise, that first evening. The drumbeats are low, slow, far away, then faster, and it becomes part of the night-song along with the rhythm of breaking waves. The beat makes my bones dance and sends shivers through my arms and legs. It's hard to sleep then, a little scary, but not bad scary. When I dream, it's in rich reds and oranges, sparks of fire. Daddy is intrigued by the *velorio* and attends one of the ceremonies. He writes about it in the article for *National Geographic*.

You enter the parlor of the house where it is being held to pause for a short prayer in front of a homemade, quite decorative altar or shrine, and to make a contribution. You pass on through the house, greeting members of the family, and on out to an enramada lit by oil-wick lamps. There are benches all around and you are immediately served a special herb-scented brew of coffee.

And then comes the music, if it can rightly be called that! It is made by two log drums, a stick rubbed on a grater, and a gourd rattle. The theme is halfway between a chant and a song, and is repeated continuously to the pounding, varying rhythms of the drums. The floor soon fills up with dancing couples of all ages. The ritual is quite unvarying. It is not "voodoo" but has its own comparative appeal and flavor. It certainly gives us an out-of-the-world feeling to wake up in the middle of the night and hear the incessant throbbing of drums in an otherwise silent tropical night.

IT STAYS MOSTLY A MYSTERY TO ME, this time of drums. My friends say *velorios* are the work of the devil; strange customs brought over by African slaves centuries ago—part Haitian voodoo and pure blasphemy. All kinds of earth spirits are worshipped, not God, not Jesus. Daisy says it's only for ignorant *heréticos*. She shakes her head and lowers her voice. "The spirits —they get agitated. I've heard of strange things that happen— people start frothing at the mouth and their eyes roll into their heads and they start speaking languages no one understands. It's not good to call up the spirits like that. Not that I believe in them." When she finds out Daddy went to a *velorio*, she crosses herself and says she'll say a rosary for him. I never learn the purpose of it all, or what spirits are being prayed to, in the smoky firelight. I just know it wakes some flame inside me, something hot and burning, that makes me restless. *Ba boom, ba boom, ba boom.*

It seems that the only things I can count on might be the earth spirits; at least the ones that bring trade winds and rain that wakens seeds below the surface to pierce through the hard ground and face the sunlight. It's also the same rain that pounds everything into submission, like Daddy's deluges of stinging words. Still, we shake off the muck and face the sunlight every day, even if it's all we have to look forward to.

Earth spirits or not, the drumbeats slowly fade as Miches gets electrical power. It's part of Trujillo's plan to modernize the country, but the generator breaks down so frequently everybody keeps their kerosene lanterns in the same places they've always hung—just in case. But gradually nights grow ever noisier. Radios wash over the evening sounds, drowning the croak of frogs, the whistle of night birds, and the slapping of waves. And in June, when the drums of the *velorio* begin, the drumbeats are faint, far away, no longer the heartbeat of the night. Now it's the spirits—and our own heartbeats—getting battered.

There's nothing we can do to stop the onslaught of night noise when Miches becomes electrified twenty-four hours a day. Mama stows away the kerosene lanterns for the nights we have power outages, but those are few. Maria Antonia's bar gets a new jukebox and the bar up in the hills gets an even louder one. A couple of radio stations join the fray. Now our evenings are shrill with thumping notes that silence the frogs' guttural symphony, the swish of palm fronds, and the splash of waves. The fragile web of nature sounds that used to calm Daddy is now just a faint backdrop to the assault, which closes in on Casalata with a force that agitates Daddy even more than usual.

Berta says it serves him right; that his past job is catching up with him here. I don't understand what she means, so she explains. Our father, the electrical engineer who installed hydroelectric power dams in poor countries before he became a coconut farmer, is now at the mercy of electrical power himself. She whispers that it was dumb of him not to know electricity would come to Miches, that of course everything would get noisier. All I know is that nights are worse now, even if we all stuff cotton in our ears and wrap pillows around our heads.

Daytime is safety—a time when I can wrap myself in morning light and once again hear the muffled music of morning: the slow *lap lap* of waves, a rooster crowing, some barking dogs, the rattle of the milk vendor's can, and the clop of horses' hooves on the path outside our gate. It's all flavored with the scent of orange blossoms and Mama's cooking pots on the stove. It's when I can breathe easier and try to forget a torturous night. But one day the safety disappears at dawn when a loud clatter startles us from sleep. A thief, just a young boy, has tried to get into our bathroom window. Daddy grabs his arms and yells at Mama to get the police, who come and take the would-be robber away. The kid has cut himself on the sharp aluminum bathroom sill, and when he's released after a few days, he spreads a story about how Daddy actually beat him with a chain.

There is no logic to the boy's story, but it catches fire like a piece of dry straw and spreads all through Miches. Now my friends ask me what really happened, "Did your father actually go crazy and do that?" It gets worse when the village police decide they need to have a court hearing to "find the facts" of the case, since the boy's father has decided to sue Daddy for beating his son in the pasture. So we appear before the town judge. Daddy says, "This is nuts, what the hell are we doing here? We're the goddamn victims for Chrissakes!"

The air is still and muggy, and sweat and fear trickle down my armpits. Berta and Mama are wearing dresses for the occasion. Daddy looks worried in his blue cotton shirt and khaki pants. He keeps shaking his head and repeating "This is nuts." Mama's eyes are anxious, her skin pale. She fiddles with a strand of hair that has escaped its clip. Daddy sits straight up and he's holding Mama's hand. I can tell he's simmering with anger. I expect it will show up this night, at home, with a drunken rage. But it's too early in the day to worry about that so I daydream about being in the United States where nothing like this could ever happen, and where no one would notice us anyway, because we look just like them. The judge agrees it would be impossible for the kid to be telling the truth, but he decides to fine Daddy anyway for allowing the boy to injure himself on the window frame. Daddy practically jumps out of the seat, but then sits down again, silent. As we escape the stifling mob in the building and step into the midday heat, I feel lightheaded and unbalanced, my heart a loud drumbeat. I stumble and Berta rights me. It seems impossible that anyone can possibly believe Daddy would beat a helpless child with a chain. Daddy's beatings are with words, not with chains.

Chapter Nine

❋

Portrait of a Birthday

It's my birthday today. I was to have an afternoon party, but Daddy started drinking early, so I have to get on my bicycle and ride through town until I find all of my friends and tell them the party is off because Daddy's sick. They know what I really mean. He's already known as *el Americano loco*, so these outbursts don't seem to bother others too much. Niña gives me an extra hug and tells me she'll say a rosary for us.

It's now nighttime. Daddy's shorts hang on his hipbones like clothes threatening to slide slowly off a wire hanger. The khaki sags in front down to a vee below his belly. Tobacco-brown skin sends out the faint smell of stale sweat, rum, and smoke. I watch as the cigarette glued by spittle to his lower lip bobs and sheds ashes as he talks at us, to us, or in spite of us. I don't understand these rants—this time he's mad at the company that buys our copra and the trucking company, which is two weeks late in picking up the latest crop. Another forgotten cigarette burns a shallow grave in the flat arm of his chair next to his drink. The rug by his feet is pocked with burn holes. Large hands push through thinning hair and then swoop in wild arcs, almost knocking off the glass of rum.

I stare past him at the large *National Geographic* map of the world. It takes up the entire wall behind his chair. It's filled with pushpins—red for places he's been to by himself, blue for travels with Mama, and white ones for the whole family. The llama rug, a large carved gourd, and a phonograph record of Andean flute music are from a blue-pushpin time— the two years Daddy and Mama spent in the Peruvian Andes just after they got married. Under the map, a bookcase is filled with weary paperbacks, a mongrel collection of Zane Grey Westerns and mysteries mostly by Earl Stanley Gardner (no relation to us). Yellow lamplight carves deep shadows under Daddy's nose. He made the lamp base from a coconut. The shade is a sheet of coco fiber wrapped around a wire frame. I shift my eyes slightly and lose myself in the swirling pattern cast by the tightly woven fibers. I try to look as if I'm paying attention to Daddy without seeing him at all, just waiting for him to exhaust himself. Eventually he will; only then will Berta and I be allowed to go to bed.

Mama slumps over the dining room table in her chair. She smokes and watches him with narrow eyes, sometimes cringing. She doesn't look at us, frozen in our seats at this now almost nightly ritual. Daddy's eyes darken. He orders Mama to make him another drink. Berta tenses near me, picking at her lip with a fingernail like she always does, sometimes until it bleeds. Her features are locked shut, hard and impenetrable. I hold my stomach with my arms as if I can protect myself that way, and I will the tears to stay inside. It's important to not call attention in any way. Daddy's voice reverberates and bounces in this house of metal walls. Crickets buzz outside, drawn by the light. I pray for the sound of frogs that precedes rain, but the swamp is quiet. I wish rain would drown him out. A good downpour will send him to bed, defeated—outshouted by nature.

But the only storm is inside these walls. I study the rug and the parade of llamas, heads held high, stepping one behind the other along the border. I watch a cigarette drop and smoke itself out on the cement floor. It misses the rug this time. I'm drowning with anger that has nowhere to go—so it stays a dull pain inside, burrowing deep. My eyes sting from trying to stay awake. I'm waiting for the end of this one, just waiting for the squall to pass. Not a good birthday; just another bad night in Miches.

The next morning, Daddy is especially quiet and sits with his coffee on the front porch. I avoid him as much as I can, but have to face him at the breakfast table. He brushes a limp strand of hair from his forehead. "I was just blowing off steam," he says. "You know that's all it is. Come here." He pulls me into his lap and gives me a smoky kiss on the head. "You're my favorite," he says quietly, so no one else will hear. I squirm and tell him I have chores to do, so he lets me go.

Mama gathers her mending and takes her coffee into their bedroom. She sits by the window in silence, attacking the sewing pile. Her fingers guide the needle in and out, in and out, as if somehow she can fix everything that's wrong by patching worn fabric and sewing on missing buttons. She winces once when she pricks her finger. She sees me in the doorway with a book in hand and musters a half-smile. "Finished with your history lesson?" she asks.

Tonight, when Daddy's exhausted himself from yelling again—this makes two nights in a row—when we're finally allowed to go to bed, Berta stands in front of the bedroom mirror and picks at pimples until they bleed as I crawl under the mosquito netting that's tucked around our beds. When the room goes dark I can hear her sniffle into the pillow.

I can't tell if I'm dreaming, but it's past midnight when I hear a strange noise coming from the other bedroom. It sounds almost like crying, but it's not Mama. Berta is asleep. The sound fades as the front door creaks open on its metal hinges, and now I can tell Mama's getting out of bed too, following the noise outside. Then there's a long, strange wail, a low sound that seems to be coming from some dark place far off. I shake Berta until she mumbles "What, *what?*"

I try to tell her something bad is happening outside, but all I can do is whisper "I'm scared," and then she can hear it too.

She takes my hand and we tiptoe as far as the front door and peek out. My heart is throbbing and her hand is holding mine so tight it hurts. There's a three-quarter moon, and it is light enough to see Daddy on his knees out by the front gate. Mama is kneeling next to him, saying something we can't hear. He pushes her away and just stays there, planted on the ground, crying. The night goes still and now we can hear his words, not the usual yelling, just this strange moan.

"Just get me a rope, Emily. Get me a goddamn rope." His voice rises, and breaks. "Let me kill myself; I just want to die."

Berta flinches; I can barely breathe. Lightning rushes through my body, jolts of electricity, bolts of danger. We cling together by the doorway, paralyzed with fear. Mama moves closer to Daddy and puts her arms around him. He pushes away. "It's all been a mistake, the biggest damn mistake in my life."

She hushes him. "No, no, no. Don't say that. You don't mean it." He slumps against her and they sway together, cry together, under the pale light of the moon.

"What do we do?" I ask Berta, my teeth chattering so hard I bite my tongue.

"Nothing. He's not going to do anything."

"But—"

Her voice is small, hard as a rock. "He won't. You hear? He just won't."

We stand there, half-hidden behind the door, and watch as Mama and Daddy rock back and forth and his cries get smaller and smaller until all we can hear is Mama saying "Everything will get better, honey. Everything will be all right. We'll make it."

A frog croaks off in the distance, and another answers. A cricket screeches over by the lagoon, and a mosquito circles our faces, looking for a landing spot. Daddy staggers to his feet, and Mama holds his arm. They begin to walk slowly back to the house. Berta propels me toward our room. "Hurry," she whispers. "They can't ever know we saw anything."

The next morning, Mama makes coffee as usual, but Daddy stays in bed.

"Just a touch of the *gripe*," Mama says. A cold. He sleeps until lunchtime and Mama takes a tray into the bedroom. He gets up after siesta, saying he's feeling better. He showers and heads down the path to his workshop. He doesn't drink at all that night, but I can barely sleep. A weight settles into my chest and pins me down in the bed until I think I'm suffocating. I keep seeing Daddy crouching on the ground, begging for a rope to hang himself with. I decide if I'm really good, and never make Daddy mad at me, then he won't ever think like that again.

BERTA DOESN'T EVER TALK much anyway, but after this episode she gets even quieter, at least at home. She buries herself in books for hours at a time, alone at a far corner of the yard, or gets in the ocean. In this place of no escape, Berta swims in the bay almost every day, paralleling the wave breaks all along the shore, diving and turning and floating. She grows tan and tall alone in the water, close to the deep where shark fins thread the surface and sting rays fly below. I stay close to shore, where my feet can find bottom, and worry when Berta is so far away she's just a speck that I lose between waves.

"No wonder she's a good swimmer," Daddy says. "Her feet are as big as flippers."

At thirteen, Berta's feet are already too big to fit into women's shoes, so she wears men's sneakers. She towers over most Dominicans and tends to slump her back so her height isn't as noticeable. But in the ocean she becomes fishlike, as graceful as a mermaid. I'm glad she can't hear Daddy's remark. He's always criticizing her for something or another, like the time her bicycle chain came off the sprocket and she couldn't figure out how to fix it. Mama doesn't say anything when Daddy talks like that. When Berta's not in the water, or studying her lessons, she reads and listens to the portable radio we are only allowed to turn on for short periods of time, because we have to save the batteries in case a hurricane threatens.

She doesn't let Daddy hug her anymore, not the way he still pulls me up into his lap. I think she's mad because he won't let her curl her hair. But she's been upset at him for a long time, so maybe it's something else. She reminds me of a hermit crab that way, scooting into a shell whenever he's nearby. She has wary blue eyes and thick blond hair that flashes gold when she brushes it in the sun. She doesn't think she's pretty, but she likes her shiny hair. She wants to grow it long, but Daddy won't let her. Mama cuts our hair outdoors, always the same way. Bangs just above the eyebrows, and straight across under our ears. When Berta is older she pleads with Mama to let it grow, so she does until the night Daddy yells at her that long hair isn't practical and besides which, what the hell is she trying to do, show it off for Miches boys, huh? Berta just looks down and shakes her head no.

Lately she doesn't like me to tag along when she visits her friends, but since their younger sisters are my pals, we often end up together at the same house for a fiesta, or, like today, when we're going to a birthday party. We wear identical dresses, which don't fit right anymore since we got them two birthdays ago. On the way home, Berta crosses over to the other side of the street.

"Why are you mad at me?" I yell across the roadway.

"I'm not—just leave me alone." We walk in silence.

"What did I do?" I complain.

"You just bug me. It makes me sick when you kiss up to Daddy. You're always asking him to explain stuff." She says it like it's dirty or disgusting. That's true, I do ask him some things, like how to mix different colors of paint to get the just the right shades, or where hurricanes come from, or why the frogs always croak when it rains. I think I'm trying to make up for the fact I'm not the boy he wanted; a boy who can fix bicycle tires and broken boat engine parts. I only talk to Daddy when he's sober, and he seems to like that. Besides, this way he won't kill himself—but I don't tell Berta that.

"I'm just curious," I say, mimicking Mama the time I asked her why she likes looking up unusual words in the dictionary. Of course Mama also says learning fancy words helps her beat Daddy at Scrabble. When Berta ignores me, I pester her even more. She complains to Mama, who tells me to leave my sister alone. However, when it's just the two of us, adrift in the pitching surf of Daddy's rage, I think somehow that Berta will protect me if things get unbearable—even if we can't walk on the same side of the street. I cling to the thought as if it will be true, as if it will stop me from drowning in fear.

Chapter Ten

❋

Nightmare

"Wake up, girls." Mama's urgent voice interrupts my dream. I cling to sleep as if it's a life vest that will save me, but it's no use. Mama has already moved the mosquito netting aside and now pulls me up to a sitting position. A jukebox blasts the stillness of the night. Daddy's letter-writing campaign for silence after 10 p.m. didn't work. The police chief just shrugs and says no laws are being broken, the *comandante* at the military post says he has no authority, and the *alcalde*, the town mayor, is an investor in the newest bar.

I know what this wake-up call means even before Mama whispers, "Your father says we're going to the *finca*." Even with ears stuffed with cotton, Daddy has woken up.

"What time is it?" I mutter. Berta is groaning awake in the bunk below me.

"Late. It doesn't matter. Don't keep your father waiting." She switches the light on. "Fifteen minutes," she warns. Berta rubs her eyes and stumbles to the bathroom.

Daddy is crashing about in their bedroom and yelling. "I can't STAND it!" he booms, knocking a glass off his dresser. Mama shushes him, tells him we'll be ready to go in a jiffy. She scours the refrigerator and pantry for food for tomorrow and fills a cloth bag with the findings.

We travel up the coast in our open skiff, Daddy steering from the rear seat. Bobby balances at Daddy's feet to stay dry, near the ten-horsepower Johnson outboard mounted on the stern. The middle seat is for Mama and Berta. I sit in a narrow vee in the bow, along with the anchor and a coil of rope. Keeping the motor running is a challenge since there are no engine parts locally available. I worry it will stall out mid-journey—a scary proposition, as Daddy would have to remove the cover and troubleshoot as we drift. When this happens, I'm always afraid we'll float away into open ocean or be overturned by breaking waves.

The bay is full of sharks, moray eels, stingrays, and other dangerous creatures. In the daytime we watch out for the darker color of the water that can signal a concealed reef, but at night we travel blind. Motoring out around the mouth of the Yeguada River is tricky too, because here the bay fills with river silt and water depth changes dramatically. Once past the Yeguada, it's a straight stretch toward the *finca*, but at night it's hard to spot our property among the long fringe of coconut palms that line the entire coast to Punta Hicaco. We used to have a dock at the *finca*, but storms washed it away regularly and eventually Daddy gave up rebuilding it. Tonight the bay is calm. At least the rivers aren't running high, flooding down from the mountains pushing logs, dead cows, or other debris out into the bay—more obstacles we could run into in the dark.

Our skiff is a dark shadow on a black sea. I hold tight to the sides of the boat as if I can keep it from falling apart that way, keep myself from falling apart. Cocoloco is about four kilometers away by land, and the boat ride takes about forty minutes. The shoreline at night is an unbroken blur of beach and the spiky silhouettes of coconut fronds. Our small *finca* house is concealed behind a break of trees. Shivering with salt spray and fright, I strain my eyes trying to find landfall from my perch on the bow, but all I can see are vague shapes, which is true even on the clearest of nights. Finally we get near enough to see the tin roof reflecting the light of the moon and we navigate by that.

When we get close to shore, Daddy swings the boat into the breaking waves and we jump out and scramble to the sandy beach. He anchors the boat away from the breakers and swims ashore, followed by Bobby. Stars twinkle like jewels and the moon pierces the darkness with light. Ahead of me, fireflies dart in and out of the shadows of the sea grape bushes. I tremble in relief and cold. Looking back at the faint light to the west that is Miches, I'm sure everyone there has been sound asleep for hours, even as jukeboxes blare into the night. There's no electric power in the *finca*, except when Daddy runs the generator to dry copra.

The flashlight glances along the dirt path leading to the fenced clearing and the wooden hut on stilts. I stay very close to Mama and Berta, putting my feet where they step to keep out of the way of land crabs and tarantulas. Exhausted by the effort of getting to the finca, Daddy is now sober and tired. The only sounds here are the rustle of the young coconut palms all around us and the splash of waves. At least now Daddy will sleep. When we unlock the upstairs room, I sigh in relief and climb into the sanctuary of my bunk—after a flashlight search for tarantulas or centipedes, because sometimes they sneak in even though the room is screened. Mama pulls out the chamber pot we can use inside just for peeing. Otherwise, we have to take the dark path to the outhouse. I can wait until morning. I don't want to battle any more crabs and spiders, especially by myself. The clock says 1:35 a.m. It's been a long night for a short sleep.

The next morning, after I finish my chores, Bobby and I head into the *finca* backcountry, stopping by a stream to watch pollywogs wiggle around, and then follow a cloud of butterflies until they disappear. I come across workers pulling coconuts off the tree with long poles that have sharp hooks at the end. They wave at me. They're used to my comings and goings. Another group is husking the coconuts by quick pushes on sharp spikes that are stuck in the ground. The outer husks are left in the field to rot and become fertilizer. The piles of nuts are loaded into saddlebags on the back of three horses and a donkey. I follow behind as the laden animals make their way to a group of sheds by the beach. Here the bags are unloaded right beside the men who chip off the hard shell with machetes to remove the fresh coconut meat. The tin-roofed building is buzzing with flies, sweat, and the sound of chipping.

Coconut shell chips fuel the big copra dryer. When we're at the finca, Berta and I take turns helping Daddy shovel chips into the furnace so he can rest. Berta sees me as she clangs the metal door shut and sets down the shovel.

"Oh, good—it's your turn," she says, wiping her forehead. "I'm going for a swim. Daddy should be back in a few minutes."

The furnace crackles and sparks fly through the cracks of the heavy door. The building is screened in to let in the ocean breeze, but the hot air that funnels from the furnace to the commercial drier makes my skin all sticky. Daddy operates the drier from sunup to sundown; it turns five thousand fresh nuts into copra in two days. Every few minutes I open the creaky door and shovel in piles of chips. I always have a book nearby to pass the time, so I'm startled when Daddy shows up. He musses up my hair, as if last night's nightmarish trip didn't even happen. I guess it's not a nightmare for him.

"Whatcha reading?"

I pick up the paperback and show him the title. It's a Zane Grey Western. Daddy imitates a gunfighter pulling out his weapon in a fast draw, and it's funny so I laugh. He picks up the shovel and I stick the book in my pocket.

"See you later, alligator," he says.

"After a while, crocodile."

When evening falls we gear up for one of Daddy's favorite rituals, which takes place along the winding trails of the *finca*—the hunt for dinner. Armies of land crabs forage in the sandy soil of Cocoloco. Twelve inches long and anywhere from khaki-brown to silver-blue in color, the males are the scariest. One of their pincers is the size of a child's hand, my hand. The inner parts of the claw are serrated and sharp, strong enough to pierce a young coconut. We head out in a drizzle, each of us armed with a flashlight, a cloth sack, and some kind of blunt instrument. Mine is a small hoe. The night crowds in around us as we slosh single file through the mud, our sneakers soaked just minutes into the trek. We aim our flashlights like guns as we squish-slide, slip-step. Daddy leads the way, followed by Mama and me. Berta brings up the rear because I'm too afraid to be the last one, where the blackness swallows up everything behind us. The rule is the first person to spot a crab is to stop and alert the rest of the family.

"I see one!" Mama shouts. She points to a large crab frozen momentarily by the light. It scuttles from side to side, its pincers waving like a boxer in the ring and its protruding eyes swiveling on their stems. Berta lifts her shovel and whacks at it until it stops moving. Daddy helps lift the oozing creature, careful to pick it up from the back, away from the claws, just in case it isn't really dead yet. He flips it into Mama's sack and we move on. I'm lucky, this night I don't have to be a killer. Even so, I have to carry my share of the bounty. After we've bagged enough we head back home, where Berta lights the Coleman lantern and Mama gets the big pot of water boiling on the camp stove. Daddy hacks away at the crabs, removing the guts and hard outer shell. He pulls each pincer off separately—the prize, packed full of meat. Berta pumps the well and rinses off the whole mess. I set the picnic-style table with plates and nutcrackers, the big metal kind with hinges. Dry and safe in the circle of the hissing lantern, we settle in for the feed. After dinner, Berta and I haul the carcasses to the compost pile, where the sun will bleach the growing mound into the color of ashes, the pallor of death.

Chapter Eleven

※

First Sight

t's fly-swatting weather, muggy and still. The trade winds are holding their breath for a change, as if waiting for a sign they can exhale. It's the summer before Berta will leave for high school in Florida, since she's now finished all the correspondence courses available. We make a trip to the capital to buy her some new clothes and finish preparing for her trip to the US. We'll meet with my parents' friends, Norma and Ed Breeden. Expatriates like us, they live in Ciudad Trujillo in a house on a street with shaded sidewalks in the American colony. Colony children go to the American School and wear pretty clothes. I think this is what life in the States will be like for Berta too.

With Berta gone, I'll have our bedroom all to myself. I wish I could go with her. But I'm only twelve, and I have to wait before I get my chance—a lifetime away. I make her promise to write me often, so I can imagine my way through the years I have to endure. It will be like when I used to play with my doll Diana and I'd make up another childhood, the one I wanted to have but didn't. I'd spend hours under the bunk bed, where I made a dollhouse from a box. I named Diana after the goddess of hunt from an old book on mythology. I'm too old for dolls now.

When we enter Ciudad Trujillo the *público* honks its way to the Hotel Presidente, where a large portrait of Trujillo stares down from a wall. *El Jefe's* chest is a blur of medals, from his shoulders all the way to his waist, and he looks like a picture of a medieval king from one of my history books. When I squint, his face comes into focus. *El Jefe's* eyes gaze out across the room as if he's watching us. His lips are smiling, but his eyes look dead, like the fish I caught after it writhed and then became very still. Mama pulls me away and we take the creaky elevator up to our rooms. These trips to the capital are the only times that Berta and I are in a room with a real door instead of a flimsy curtain between us and our parents' room. Berta opens the window and we look down two stories to the street, where men in *guayabera* shirts carry briefcases and women click along in high heels. I imagine they're window shopping at stores where mannequins model the latest fashions direct from *Nueva York*. Peddlers hawk lottery tickets on street corners, competing to sell winning numbers. A fruit vendor pulls a cart full of peeled oranges and chunks of pineapple, calling out "*Naranjas dulces, piñas.*"

After we've unpacked, we have lunch at a Chinese restaurant across the street. Daddy orders a variety of dishes so we all can try something different. Dessert is a very un-Chinese dish of watery flan. Daddy and Mama are talking about new political unrest here in the capital, where students from the university are staging anti-American rallies. Apparently the US government recently spoke harshly of the Trujillo regime, and the local papers are filled with letters to the editors denouncing the *Yanqui imperialistas* and their lies about the beloved Benefactor.

We take a taxi to the Breedens' apartment. When Daddy gives the driver the address, the man frowns and says we should be careful; there's been some trouble near the US Embassy. Ed Breeden greets us and waves to his wife Norma, who's sitting with a group of other Americans around a television set. No one is smiling, but she leaps up and gives us hugs. Norma is a nervous and jumpy type, pretty in a sharp Joan Crawford kind of way—all edges and angles. Ed is large and quiet and speaks softly.

Norma says Trujillo is furious that President Eisenhower has made a statement condemning his actions and charging the Dominican government with corruption. So now *El Jefe* is on television, his voice high and angry, his arms pumping up and down and making his medals shake.

He looks like the hotel portrait, but smaller and fatter. The adults are paying attention to the broadcast, but I'm intrigued by the television itself, the first one I've ever seen. I worm my way through the chairs and find a spot on the floor directly in front of the cabinet and settle down to watch. Mama tugs at my arm and pulls me aside. "You're blocking everyone's view. Come back and sit with your sister."

I retreat to the back of the room and Norma comes over, fussing. "Rita, you're welcome to join us—why don't you sit in one of the chairs?"

"Because I can't see the television from here."

"What do you mean?" Norma's voice rises. "Emily, have you ever had her eyes tested?"

"No, of course not," Mama says. "She does her lessons just fine, and reads all the time." I suddenly remember the beach game we play in Cocoloco, the one where Daddy tells us to count the number of boats we see on the horizon. I can never see any of them unless they're right near shore, so my answers are always wrong and Daddy gets mad at me.

Norma and Mama move into the kitchen to talk, and I sink into a *Life* magazine, full of colorful ads for new Chevrolet cars, Camel cigarettes, and other exotic things to buy. Norma comes out with a tray of cookies. "I've talked your mother into letting you go to our eye doctor tomorrow. I think you just need glasses." I take a cookie and nod politely, but I don't like doctors because they give you shots that hurt. I hope Mama forgets to make the appointment.

The Breedens take us out to dinner that night to a restaurant famous for Spanish *paella*. "It takes an hour to prepare," Norma says as we're seated, "but oh God is it good!" She often talks in exclamation points.

Berta and I dig into our food, and are surprised when there's a sudden silence at our table and then Norma's voice cuts through the quiet. "But of course you will!" she almost shouts at Daddy. Norma is not afraid of Daddy, not at all. I catch my breath when she fires off at him just as loudly as he does to us. He gets a certain glint in his eye when they spar, almost like two roosters at a cockfight. Mama will never talk back to Daddy. I can only remember the one time when she did. I don't know what Daddy said to her, but Mama's voice suddenly rose from a squeak to a howling torrent of words that got louder, bouncing back from the metal walls. I hid behind the kitchen door.

Daddy turned red and raised his fist as if he was going to hit her, and she stopped, as if a switch turned off.

Then from Daddy, a chilling, low growl, no yelling, just words bitten off sharply, one after the other. *"Don't—you—ever —do—that—again!"* I watched, horrified, as Mama crumpled back into herself, her outrage hanging in the air like a thunderhead.

But here's Norma Breeden snapping and barking at Daddy, and he just laughs. She continues to lean right in Daddy's face. I look at Mama, who hasn't said a word; it's almost like she's scared of Norma, too.

I hold my breath. Norma is practically yelling now: "You people need a real vacation—for Chrissakes, you haven't been home for how many years? Get the hell out of here for a coupla weeks. Jesus, Jesse. The coconuts aren't going anywhere!"

Right there, that night, it's decided, just like that. Our whole family will go to Florida and drop Berta off with friends of the Breedens' who will take her to her new school. Mama and Daddy and I will fly up to New York for a whole week with our relatives. When the Breedens drop us off at the hotel I hug Norma, even with her vodka breath. "You poor child," she mutters so only I can hear, but I don't know what she means.

I barely sleep that night. A pang of worry thunders through my chest as I wonder if Daddy will change his mind about this tomorrow, when he's sober. But he doesn't. We extend our stay in the capital, and Daddy scurries to all the proper agencies to get our visas. Mama and I take a taxi to Norma's eye doctor. After all the tests, he takes my mother aside. When she comes back she says, "Apparently you have extreme nearsightedness. I had no idea." I get to choose a frame, and I pick black rims that rise to a cat's-eye point at either side. We return two days later for my new glasses. I don't know what to expect. I keep my eyes closed when they're fitted, and then I blink, then blink again, and almost jump out of the chair.

I can see the pores of the doctor's skin, and individual strands of hair. I close my eyes again then open them and find I can see all the way to the other side; there's Mama smiling. Her lips, freshly coated with Revlon's "Fire and Ice," are bright red.

I'm speechless and walk gingerly across the floor, almost afraid to take steps, as if I might trip on the air itself. Everything has sharp color and distinct shape. I pick up a magazine and start to bring it up close to my face—but now I don't have to do that. I open the door to the street and it's almost too much to bear. No longer just blurs, cars, people, trees all have edges and beginnings and endings.

Back at the hotel, Berta and I stay up at night watching the square below, brilliant with neon and the red and yellow of car lights. A misty rain comes in and transforms the street into reflections as pretty as Mama's costume jewelry, facets winking and changing color with splashes and spatters. The next morning at breakfast, Daddy reads an article aloud to Mama from *El Caribe*. It's an article denouncing all the lies the Americans are spreading about Trujillo. This article mentions a Dominican writer who supposedly helped the Yankees spread lies. He's been discovered in a dry riverbed, burned to death in his car. There seem to be an awful lot of burned cars that make the news these days. Just like the article about the American pilot a year or two ago, the paper reports it as an accident, saying Trujillo sent a huge wreath and public condolences to his family. Daddy and Mama say little about this report. Their silence is almost as revealing as the details of a fluttering leaf, or a speck of boat I know I'll now be able see, far away on the horizon.

Chapter Twelve

❄

Flying High

I n August we leave for the airport. Daddy's foreman will take care of Bobby while we're gone. Berta has a brand new suitcase, pearl white with brocade designs of flowers and shiny gold snaps. Mama smiles a lot. She's telegraphed Aunt Libb, her sister-in-law, who lives in the family home in Southampton. Aunt Libb is a widow. Mama's brother died one night a few years ago when a train struck his car. We learned this by telegram and Mama didn't go back to the States for the funeral. She said Daddy needed her at home. Berta says it was mean of Daddy not to let her go to see her only brother buried.

We arrive at the airport three hours early. Mama and Daddy seem nervous, as if maybe the officials won't let us leave the country for some reason. Mama is shaking as we go through all the different checkpoints, where one piece of paper or another is examined, stamped, or handed back. Guards with guns patrol the lounges and the customs area. Daddy smokes his cigarette with rapid puffs and Mama keeps wiping her forehead. I feel like I'm going to throw up from nerves and excitement. Berta is smiling to herself as if she's already left on her adventure. The Pan American airplane waits out on the tarmac, all silver and shiny. I jump up and down.

"Behave, dear," Mama warns, but she's finally smiling as we climb the metal stairs. A pretty woman in a dark blue suit hands me some chewing gum and a silver pin shaped like wings. I'm a Junior Stewardess! She shows us the paper bags we're to use if we get airsick, which Berta does soon after takeoff. I sit up straight and sip a cup of ginger ale, feeling like a grown-up. Mama and Daddy are holding hands and Berta stares out the window at the cotton-ball clouds.

The Miami airport is orderly and quiet, even with announcements bouncing off the loudspeakers every few seconds. Everything is so clean, it feels like I must be in a movie or a dream. Berta puts some coins in vending machine, and out pops a packet of cheese crackers. She hands me one of the small squares and I feel like I'm in the Catholic church and this is a communion wafer, a special sacrament. Berta laughs out loud and I join her. We snort and snuffle and hold hands until she is picked by the Breedens' friend who will drive her to the school. Mama sobs and even Daddy wipes his eyes as we leave her.

The three of us fly to New York, where Mama practically falls into her sister-in-law's arms. I can tell Mama has missed her family awfully, even though she never says anything about them. My grandmother's house on Long Island sits like a picture, under leafy trees and surrounded by lawn. The house seems anchored by the weight of history; a place where generations lived and died. Our New York relatives are not like us who flit about like mosquitoes in warm places, landing here and there and finally settling, if you can call it that, on an island with a dangerous dictator and the constant threat of hurricanes. Casalata now seems flimsy and bare compared to this solid house where Mama was born.

Inside, the hallway is dark and cool and smells of wood polish. A curve of banister beckons and I climb the stairs, made quiet by faded wool runners. A hint of mothballs follows me upstairs and triggers a faint memory of when Daddy was in between engineering jobs and we moved back to Southampton for almost a year when I was three. So this place is strange and familiar at the same time. My cousins Ann and Mary pull me into their room and suddenly I'm playing in English, talking in English, and eating American food. Memories of throwing snowballs and making snow angels float to my mind and I ask Mary, "Did we really do that?"

She says yes and fishes out some old photos. "You were the baby." In the picture we're all laughing and full of snow, but I can't remember what that kind of winter feels like.

We walk down clean streets to Hildreth's Department Store, where my grandfather worked his entire life as an accountant. Mama shows me the counter where she sold cleaners and dust mops after school. We visit my father's home a few miles across the island. My grandmother Gardner used to own the *Sag Harbor Express*, the local newspaper, and my uncle now runs the business. Daddy says my uncle isn't a good manager, and that really his wife is the one who runs the show. He says it like that is a bad thing. We go for a ride on my uncle's yacht on the Long Island Sound, just like rich people in magazine photos. Lobster pots are piled up on the shoreline and all the fences seem to be painted a clean bright white. As if nature here is swept and polished just for us. The Long Island days are green and blue and fresh and over quickly.

Much too soon we're back in the Dominican Republic, and for several weeks everything seems extra loud and dusty and dirty. I think how very odd our living style must be to any foreigner. But my friends thrill to the fancy soaps and other treats I've brought as gifts. I thought I'd be happy to have the whole room to myself, but I feel lonely without Berta, as if part of me has gone with her white suitcase. Bobby seems happy to jump into Berta's empty bed at night while I lean down and pet him from the bunk above. When he wags his bushy tail and begs me to throw sticks to chase, the loneliness goes away. Mama seems sad for the first few weeks, but then cheers up too. Daddy doesn't seem to have changed much at all. When he's drunk at night he still yells and rants, but he stops blaming me for things as much as he used to.

Soon after we get back, I paste photos of our trip into the album that Mama keeps to highlight special occasions. I like looking through the family albums, especially the one where she chronicles Berta's and my birthdays. Every year Daddy takes photographs of us individually standing in front of Mama. I flip through the pages; in this year's pictures I'm the same height as Mama, and Berta is taller than her. For the last three years, Berta and I have worn the same matching turquoise dresses each time. They fit perfectly the first year. In the photos from the following year, mine still fits fairly well, but Berta's dress is too short. In this year's picture we hardly fit into our outfits at all and Berta is frowning into the sun. Mama said we couldn't have new dresses for two years in a row because the copra prices had gone down and they couldn't afford it. The pictures are curling up and the color is fading already. I try to straighten them out before closing up the album and storing it where the sun won't bleach it any more.

But this year everything is going to be different, better and brighter. I close my eyes and imagine next summer, when Berta will come home with pretty new clothes and so many stories to tell. What she actually will bring home I can't even imagine.

Chapter Thirteen

❊

Shipwreck

The wind is high, warning of a hurricane lurking out in the Atlantic. We're up at Cocoloco today, and I'm playing at the beach with Bobby when I see a man running up from the direction of the Suarez *finca*. I figure he is one of their coconut pickers. He sees me and halts mid-stride.

"*Tu papá?*" he wheezes, out of breath. "*Donde está?*" I point back to the house, where Daddy and Mama are sitting with cups of coffee. It is about ten in the morning. I don't pay much attention to the stranger since Daddy is an expert at fixing things and is often approached by neighboring farmers for his advice or tools. But I get curious when Daddy follows the man back toward the Suarez farm. I find Mama at the house with a worried look on her face.

"What's the matter?" I ask, reaching for the cookie tin.

"There's been a shipwreck beyond Punta Hicaco. Foreigners. Your father is going to see if he can help."

The cookie drops midway to my mouth. A flutter of excitement rips through my stomach as my mother's words sink in. *A shipwreck? Castaways?* I can barely contain myself. I start to run after Daddy, but Mama calls me back, telling me it could be hours before he returns. She hands me the clam bucket. "Here, your father will want his broth when he gets back."

Sighing, I stomp to the beach and fling the bucket down. As I dig in the wet sand for clams, my mind buzzes with excitement. On the other side of Punta Hicaco there are no reefs to calm the ocean. Even in good weather large waves lunge shoreward and shallow water changes to deep just a few feet from shore, causing a fierce undertow. I know better than to swim there; it's too dangerous. But the beaches yield a lot of treasure, so I hike there a lot, pretending I'm Robinson Crusoe. Or I'm a pirate, and this is my Treasure Island. I spend hours poking under driftwood and in the dunes, finding a glass fishing float here, a perfect shell there. Once I found a bottle with a folded piece of paper inside but the message was now just a gray smudge of mildew. Last year I spotted a wooden hatch cover with Japanese writing painted on one side. Daddy found someone in the capital to translate: *Danger! If this hatch is opened, the sea will enter.* I shivered when I heard that, imagining a ship ripped apart in a storm and thinking of sailors drowning somewhere out there beyond the breakers.

And now the seas at Punta Hicaco have brought an actual shipwreck. I wait impatiently, and finally several figures emerge out of the brush and onto our beach. I race up the shore, clams forgotten. A tall, plain-looking woman with a parrot clinging to her shoulder stands next to two men, one about Daddy's age, the other much younger. They're Americans. The woman is Pat, and her bird is Paco. Rocky is the older man, all sharp angles, silver hair, and cold gray eyes. The younger man, Joe, is muscled, tan, and blond. He has a tattoo of a snake that circles his arm just above his elbow. When he smiles at me, a jolt goes through my body. I straighten up, conscious of my baggy shorts, dripping with sand, and my hair, uncombed and hacked off like a boy's. Pat tells me to put my finger out and Paco waddles up my arm. The parrot is green with black claws that dig into my skin as he climbs my shoulder. I stare at Joe.

Rocky does all the talking. He says he owns a ship salvage business, and they were towing a barge from Miami to St. Croix with their trawler. All was fine until they hit a storm system three days out of Florida. They headed southeast, hoping for protection on the Dominican coast. Just as they spotted the entrance to Samana Bay, they lost engine power and drifted east toward Punta Hicaco. A coral reef punctured the trawler's hull a few hundred yards off shore. They had barely enough time to untie the barge, which floated ashore, before the trawler sank with all their belongings. The three swam to safety and blundered through the woods until they came upon a group of farm hands, one of whom ran to find Daddy.

At lunch, Mama volunteers dry clothing and says she'll find them a place to stay in Miches. By the time night falls everyone is dry and fed and sitting on our porch with cocktails. Pat chatters nonstop, worrying out loud about Paco.

"When we started sinking, I took him out of his cage so he wouldn't drown. I don't know what happened after that, except I was lying in the sand. Next thing I know I hear a squawk and Paco's sitting on my head." She laughs, then her mouth curves downward as she caresses the bird's feathers. "He's like my only child. I hope he doesn't catch cold."

She rattles on to Mama as the men talk, smoke cigarettes, and drink more rum. It's past my bedtime, but Mama lets me stay up. I find ways to look at Joe when he's not noticing. He catches me and winks. I turn red and stare at my feet. Rocky begins to grumble about some salvage deal that went sour in Miami. Suddenly there's a flash of metal and he stands up unsteadily, waving a small pistol and shaking his head fiercely.

"If I get my hands on that S.O.B. . . ." he begins. Then, as if he suddenly remembers where he is, he tucks the gun into his pants and sits down again, mumbling an apology. Pat glares at him. I'm nailed to my seat, not sure of what to do. I'm used to seeing rifles at the *Comandante's* quarters, or revolvers hanging off the belts of military police, but never on a foreign visitor. Daddy gets up slowly and yawns, as if nothing scary just happened.

"Well, it's been a long day—let's all get a good night's sleep. Tomorrow we'll get some men to tow your boat off the reef and look at the damage."

Pat collects her parrot as Rocky finishes off his drink. Joe winks at me again and thanks Mama for dinner and the three sway off into the darkness. Mama turns to Daddy. "What are we going to do now, Jesse?"

"Don't worry. I think Rocky's just a hothead. The best thing we can do is help them get out of here as soon as possible." I go to bed, still wide awake. Daddy is just calling these people hotheads? These strangers are unlike any other visitors we've ever had. When I fall asleep, I dream of sinking boats and tattooed arms. Two days later Paco dies, and Pat weeps for days. Mama and I help her bury the bird in our yard. The barge is towed across the bay to the village dock. The trawler is raised up from the reef and hauled ashore for repair. Pat sorts out their waterlogged possessions to see what can be saved.

Mama sends me over with laundry soap and clothespins to help Pat. She is opening a suitcase when I arrive. She pries the latch open and, with a long sigh, pulls out something buried in wads of wet clothing. It's a sandal, the high heel a clear wedge with rhinestones that sparkle. The strap, now warped by seawater, is also transparent, with multicolored stones in the shape of a rose. I've never seen anything so glamorous. All I own are two pairs of sneakers and one pair of flats for special occasions.

Pat twirls the sandal around her arm, making rainbows of color on the walls. "Oh, I hope they're not totally ruined. I never should have brought them on the boat. But when I wear these I feel so—so pretty, I guess. I know it's foolish, but I just had to bring them. Now look." Her fingers tremble as she tries to smooth the twisted strap. She seems lost in her misery, so I leave the soap and go back home, thinking Cinderella's glass slipper must have looked just like that.

As the days pass, the storms blows over, but my own tropical disturbance is brewing—I've developed a big crush on Joe, and my stomach lurches when I see him. He spends most days at the dock, readying the barge for its journey. I go down there every afternoon with cookies and lemonade and breathe in the smell of his sweat. I try not to stare at his muscled tattoo or the hair on his neck, sticky with salt, as he reaches for the snack. He gulps the drink then leans over and tousles my hair as if I were still a small child, the way Mama's friends used to pinch my cheek and tell her how cute I was, as if I wasn't there.

"I made the cookies myself," I volunteer, my voice squeaking from nervousness.

"That right? Hey, they're good. You'll make a great wife when you grow up."

He snatches another one, says thanks, and turns back to his chores. That night I close my eyes and pretend I can feel strong arms pulling me to him. I'm wearing a long silk gown and the crystal sandals. We dance and he kisses me. I kiss him back, or rather my pillow, over and over until I fall asleep.

Finally the trawler is patched up and running. The night before our guests leave, we hold a farewell party at Maria Antonia's bar for everyone who's helped put the boat together or helped bring the barge to the village. Off in a corner, Rocky wraps his arm over Daddy's shoulder as if they're best friends. He gestures and whispers, and Daddy keeps shaking his head as if saying no to something. Seated next to Joe, I can feel his bare leg press carelessly against mine as he leans in to flirt with one of our neighbor's daughters who is pretty and nineteen. He doesn't even notice our bodies are touching. Later I'm awake for hours, Joe's face drifting in and out of focus. My body aches with feelings that are new and shocking, zings of sensation everywhere. But Joe is leaving tomorrow and I'll never see him again. I begin to wish we won't have any new visitors, ever, because they always leave, making me feel even more alone. It seems nothing good ever stays around.

The next morning we make a procession to the town dock. Joe picks me up and gives me a hug, and I hope he doesn't feel how I'm trembling. Pat comes over to say good-bye. "I have something for you." She reaches into a paper bag and pulls up the crystal sandals. I sputter my thanks. Moments later the trawler fires up its engine and slowly motors away, towing the barge obediently behind. I stare at Joe, who waves once then turns away to steer the boat. I clutch Pat's bag to my chest until the two vessels are just specks on the horizon, and I feel hollow and hot at the same time.

"Good riddance," Daddy mutters under his breath as we walk home. Mama gives him a curious look, but Daddy just shakes his head. "I'll explain later."

That evening the wind is entirely gone and the bay mirrors the setting sun. Sitting on our dock, I dangle my feet in the water and think about Joe while Daddy tells Mama what happened the night before. Rocky confided that his business is really insurance fraud and that he removes or sinks vessels on demand. The insurance company pays the owners for their loss, and the owners kick back a portion to Rocky. Pat isn't really his wife but a business partner, and Joe is in on this illegal activity too. On this trip the plan was for the barge to disappear from the Miami harbor and be declared sunk or lost at sea. A buyer in St. Thomas will doctor up the paperwork and resell the barge. Rocky will get another cut from that transaction.

"Can you believe the nerve of that jerk? He actually tells me this stuff."

Daddy shakes his head. "And this after all our help. He even tried to convince me to get into the game—told me I'd make more money than just growing coconuts." He takes a swig from his drink. "I guess his only comeuppance is that his own shipwreck was accidental—not on purpose. Maybe he'll think differently about doing it to others after it happened to him."

Mama murmurs something and they sit quietly, staring at the bay.

I lie back on the still-warm wooden planks. As the sky

turns from pink to purple, I fight back angry tears. Rocky's gang is nothing better than a bunch of pirates, and they lied about almost everything. That night in bed I lie awake and confused. But my thoughts don't stay entirely bleak. Even if Pat wasn't the person I thought she was, she's left behind a special gift. All I have to do is slip my toes into the Cinderella slippers and I'll feel pretty, just like she did. In the moonlight they blink up at me—shipwrecked treasures from the deep. I look at them and pretend Joe is kissing me and telling me how pretty I look in these shoes.

Mama won't let me wear them, but I won't give them away either. It's part of remembering Joe. But in time the cloth insoles separate from the plastic and curl up and stiffen. The glue that holds the rhinestones in place disintegrates and the gems fall out. Soon I can't even imagine Joe's face, except when I look at the photo album where I pasted a few pictures Daddy took with the Brownie camera when Rocky and his crew were in Miches. The pictures are small and Joe is just a tiny figure, waving from the back of the boat as they left the harbor. I take Mama's magnifying glass to see him better, but the larger image is fuzzy. I forget him entirely when summer brings shocks so big there is no room for anything else.

Chapter Fourteen

✳

The Time of Secrets

We are just waiting for Berta to arrive. It's hot and steamy, and even Bobby is lethargic. He lies around with his tongue hanging out as if he too is waiting for a change in the weather. I move my clothes out of her dresser, making room for her arrival. I'm jumpy with happiness and fluttery nerves. Berta hasn't written us much, especially lately, so I can hardly wait for all the stories she has to tell. When she arrives home, she looks upset as she greets us. I don't know why, except maybe she's not too excited to see Daddy. A vague disquiet settles in my gut, so I grab her arm and chatter nervously about everything that's happened in the past year. I take her suitcase from her and place it on her bed, which I've made up fresh just for her homecoming.

Things settle into normalcy for a few days. Bobby doesn't want to leave Berta's side. She pets him absentmindedly and he rolls over for belly rubs. At least he's happy. One afternoon I come back home after visiting friends. I put my bicycle away and walk into the house, waving a container of *dulce de leche* that Matilde's mother has made as a welcome-home present for Berta. But something's wrong. Berta is lying facedown on her bed and Daddy and Mama are just standing there. Daddy's jaw is clenched and his mouth is twisted. Mama is white. No one says a word. Berta turns her face into the pillow and waves me out of the room. I've never heard her sob like this before, and never in front of our parents. She curls into a fetal position, pulling into herself even more. Scared, I watch as Daddy lights a cigarette and stalks off to his workshop. He doesn't look at me, but mutters in a fierce whisper: "You tell her, Emily. *You* tell her."

Mama looks like she doesn't know what to do next. Her hands are shaking and her eyes skip around the room like a fly trapped in a jar. My stomach jumps with fear, with not knowing what's going on. I just know it's bad. Eventually Mama's voice comes out in a squeak. Berta has told them she's pregnant, by a boy named Scott at school in Florida. Daddy and Mama have decided Berta must go back to the States right away, marry him, and have this baby. We will make up some story to tell the village; they haven't figured that part out. But Berta will have to leave. I sink back, my neck prickly with fear. The words have trouble sinking into my brain. How could this have happened? Who is Scott? She's never mentioned him at all to me in any letters. How can she leave? Leave me? I get up but it feels like a thousand weights are clamped to my feet. I drag myself back to the bedroom, so full of confusion I don't even know what to say or ask.

Berta finally whispers to me. All I hear, over and over again, is that she didn't know what Scott was doing to her, didn't want it, couldn't stop him, and didn't know she'd get pregnant. She doesn't even like him. "I didn't know, I didn't know." She alternately cries and throws up. There is nothing I can do to help, and there is no question of disobeying Daddy's orders.

For the next few days Daddy rages and drinks far into the night. "Goddamn it," he yells. "Son-of-a-bitch! My own daughter, my own goddamn daughter, pregnant like any village whore who opens her goddamn legs to any scum who throws her a peso!" This he says to Mama when we're in our room, as if we can't hear him. Berta puts a pillow over her ears and shakes. I go numb inside, into that dark cloudy place, but my stomach aches so much I throw up. Mama is silent in the next room except for a few low moans. My vocal chords are paralyzed and stinging with pain. *She's not that!* I shout inside my head to him: *She's a good girl. Don't say those things!* I want to scream at him, hit him, hard. *Mama, stop him! Don't you see how it hurts her?* But Mama doesn't answer him, and he doesn't stop.

Mama flies to Florida with Berta to meet Scott and his family. She comes home saying she and Scott's parents have sorted out the logistics of getting these two strangers married. There's nothing more to do. I sit in the emptiness of the bedroom, surprised I can still breathe, but I have to remember sometimes how to exhale. My stomach hurts all the time. I dread facing my friends, her friends, anyone who'll ask about Berta's sudden departure, but the next day I'm spared (at least for a little while) from everybody's questions.

The village is consumed with bigger news when Fidel Castro decides to invade the Dominican Republic. An army of guerrilla fighters fly in, followed by a flotilla of boats that make landfall on the north coast. Radio Caribe announces that the Armed Forces is in control and has already killed most of the Cuban invaders. Trujillo gets on the air, promising the cowards will be eliminated within days. In Miches, busloads of soldiers in green uniforms swarm the streets. Some look like young boys who have just been yanked out of their fathers' farms. They carry guns awkwardly, big ones, with bayonets.

Daddy stops repeating horrible things about Berta and rants about the coup instead. He says it looks like they don't have a damn clue what they're doing here, but even so a group of them practice maneuvers on the beach in front of Casalata, preparing in case any more Cuban guerrillas enter by Samana Bay. I watch them as they scramble around the rocks and splay themselves onto the beach. When they're not on duty, they flock to Maria Antonia's bar or dance with the prostitutes who smell fresh game and new money. One of the soldiers tries to flirt with me. He offers me a cigarette, which I decline with a grimace. "I'm Bengala," he announces. I look at him, finally. He has green eyes and dark eyelashes. I shrug and look away down the beach where I'm heading off to be alone. He steps in front of me.

"You know, like the Bengal tigers of India," he says again. "That's my name. What's yours?" I shake my head and take off in a run. I don't want to have anything to do with boys.

Two weeks later, the coup attempt is over. As quickly as they arrived in Miches, the soldiers depart. I watch as the bus lumbers out of town. I see Bengala; he waves and I wish I felt something, anything, except the other loss, the one I can't talk about.

Berta gets married in Florida. We have an address to write to but without a telephone we rely on infrequent letters. Berta's misery shouts through the page in what she doesn't write. Her letters drip in, each less revealing than the last. Scott's parents occasionally write and so we learn their son is earning some money working at the local bait shop. Berta is selling cosmetics door to door. As summer wears on, we perfect our lies to everyone in Miches. We're surprised to learn that Berta has fallen in love and decided to get married. Questions are on everyone's lips when they greet any of us now—*How's your sister? Tell us more about her husband—how romantic for her.* And on and on and on until I feel like screaming.

I feign delight at her new circumstances, then go home to a house turned upside down with anger and suffering. My stomach pain is constant now as Daddy drinks and rants: "She made her bed, now she has to lie in it. As far as I'm concerned she's no longer a member of this family!"

Mama, battered from the assault, turns even more silent and forgetful. She leaves trails of cigarettes she's started and put down. She burns a pot of beans and overcooks the rice. Her hands shake and her eyes dart around but I can't tell what she's looking at. Daddy repaints the skiff and puts a new coat of varnish on his workshop, his face grim and lined. It's almost like he's trying to seal up and cover over everything that's blistered and bad.

I vow I'll never mention boys to my father, ever, in fear that I too will be branded a prostitute, a slut. I try my best to be invisible. It seems as if the bottom of my life has dropped out and there is no safe place to stand. Everything looks different, flat and colorless even as the sky shines bright blue and the ocean begins its restless green surge from summer storms.

Daddy once drew me a picture of a hurricane's eye, the still center looking like the hole of a doughnut, empty but surrounded by churn. "The calm is deceptive," he'd said. "And it doesn't last. It can't—the hurricane's always moving, and the eye travels with it. And then you're hit with the full impact again."

I have recurring dreams where Casalata is the eye of the hurricane. I'm in my bed and the sheets are strangling me so I can't move. I scream out Berta's name but no sound comes out, and she's the only one running, running away. I try to tell her she has to stay, but she vanishes into the black of the surrounding storm.

We have a near-miss during hurricane season, but the storm veers upward into the Atlantic, bringing only some wild surf and two days of heavy rains. I want the storm to hit; I want the full fury. I want something to fight, or really something to be protected from, and someone to protect me.

Chapter Fifteen

❋

The Disappearance

Berta gives birth to a baby boy and names him Mitch. We learn this by letter weeks later. No pictures come, no joyful reports. On a spring morning a barefoot boy delivers a telegram, hovering around until Mama fetches a tip and sends him on his way. Telegrams are infrequent and always bear bad news. The last one we received was several years ago when one of my uncles in New York died. This one is from Berta's in-laws, requesting that we phone them as soon as possible. Nothing else. Mama walks the kilometer to the town's makeshift telephone office. At lunchtime she's still gone. Daddy says I should go see what the hell's going on; I think he just wants to eat. I'm hungry too as I wheel my bicycle down the bumpy street.

There's some kind of commotion in front of the telegraph office. Mama is kneeling in the dirt and two women are trying to pull her up. I drop the bicycle and run to her. The ladies say she was on the *teléfono* and then she started screaming and ran outside and fell. Mama just cries "no, no, no," over and over. I don't know what to do. One of the women brings a glass of water and a red parasol. I try to shade Mama. Finally she sits up and pulls me to her and whispers that we have to go home now. She dusts herself off and I can see she's still unsteady. Her shin is scraped and bleeding and she doesn't seem to notice the flies buzzing around her leg. The ladies bring a cloth but Mama waves them away, saying she's fine.

"What's wrong?" I squeak through a tight throat.

She shakes her head. "Not here." We walk in thick silence. I'll get the bicycle later. I hold Mama's hand—something we never do. It's clammy and cold. When we get home, she falls against Daddy and starts talking, so low I can hardly hear her. Daddy for once is quiet. He lights a cigarette and hands it to her.

BERTA HAS DISAPPEARED and has been missing for over two weeks. Scott's parents didn't contact us sooner because they thought it might just be a marital spat and that Berta would come back, but it's been too long, and do we know anything? This is what we learn: Berta's husband came home for lunch one day in between school and his afternoon job and found the baby asleep in the crib. The infant had recently been changed and fed, but Berta was gone. No note, nothing. Just gone. The parents took the baby boy home with them and are now caring for him, still thinking Berta might return at any time. They've filed a missing persons report and the local police have been called in. That's all anyone can do. There is no evidence of foul play. Just wait and see if she comes back. She probably will, they say. Lover's spat, most likely. They promise to telegraph us as soon as they hear anything. No, there doesn't seem to be any reason for us to fly to Florida, they are happy to take care of the baby for the time being—he's a sweet one, she says; he's used to his grandma. He'll be fine.

The shock is so great I retreat into dense numbness. Mama becomes a pale shell, almost a ghost of herself. Daddy decides we'll tell no one anything. Berta will come back to her baby, all will be fine. We just have to be patient and wait. Daddy drinks even more heavily, but instead of exploding at us he falls into a stupor, and Mama is able to get him to bed most nights; his snores keep me awake for hours. When I finally fall asleep, it's to nightmares. Berta's calling for me, but I can't see her, can't find her.

Mama keeps saying we'll get good news soon enough. Nothing we can worry about. But she fidgets and trembles, and her hair starts falling out. I find gray strands choking the shower drain. She and Daddy smoke cigarettes one after the other, leaving burning stubs forgotten. They send up smoke signals, distress calls. I snuff them out.

A month goes by and then a letter arrives from Berta's in-laws with a newspaper clipping inside. A young woman's body has been found floating in the Gulf somewhere on the west coast of Florida. The body is so decomposed that it is impossible to identify except they know she was blonde, and that her approximate age was seventeen or eighteen. Scott's parents don't know if it is Berta, but since the description does fit, they've decided we should at least be aware of the news story. They reassure us that, in any case, they've decided to adopt the baby.

Everything goes blank, except for the one thing I am

ordered to do. Daddy decides to keep up the pretense in the village. So within our family, now shriveled to three—we know what we've been told, but to the rest of the world we are to say Berta is happy in Florida.

Yes, Señora de La Cruz, the baby's growing up fine. No, Don Elpidio, I don't know why she forgets to send pictures. Yes, Juanita, maybe this year they'll come home for Christmas, but it's hard for her husband to get away from his job, you understand?

Chapter Sixteen

❋

Just a Case of Nerves

A few mornings later I wake up to a strange silence. In my pajamas, I open the curtain and look out in the kitchen. No Mama. I don't remember a day she hasn't been up at dawn to start the coffee. Mornings hum with certain sounds and smells, comforting ones even in this despair. The toasted bite of fresh coffee, a hint of tobacco smoke, and the faint metallic creak as Mama opens the kitchen door to the morning breeze. But not today. The kitchen is empty. Daddy is pacing in the living room, looking pale under his weathered tan.

"Your mother is sick," he says. I peer into their bedroom and Mama is just lying there, staring at the wall, not even looking out the window at the singing birds in the orange tree.

Daddy brings the thermometer but she turns her head away and clamps her mouth shut.

I squeak out "Mama?" as chills run up and down my spine. She blinks, and then starts to cry, little whimpers that sound faint and far away. I twist my hands and arms until I'm like a pretzel. I take a jagged breath. I must be strong, must do something, so I brew the coffee when all I want to do is scream and scream until I crumple. Daddy talks to Mama in a low tone. I can't hear what he's saying, but he comes into the kitchen and tells me to bicycle down to the *clínica* and have someone come to look at her.

"She'll be all right," he says, but I can tell by his eyes he's worried.

It's still early morning and the clinic won't be open yet, but the doctor lives next door to it, so I pedal as fast as I can. No one is on the street except the milk vendor and his donkey. Two metal vessels rock in their makeshift saddle as they make their way to Juan Kair's store. I pass the bakery and the smell of yeast floats by. At the other end of town, by the church, I knock on the door of the doctor's house. I can see his wife—burning *carbón*, the local firewood—in the outside kitchen. She comes over to where I'm standing, shaking in my sandals. The doctor has been out in the *campo* since last night attending to a farmer who lost three fingers in a machete accident.

"I'll get the nurse to come to your house," she says. I don't move. "Don't worry," she assures me again. "I'll go now and find her."

A nurse comes within the hour. Her name is Livia and she sits with Mama until the doctor gets back into town. I scramble some eggs and Daddy and I sit at the table, eating in silence. We can hear Livia murmuring to Mama. I think it must just be a touch of *gripe*. But the nurse has managed to take her temperature, and it's normal. *Nervios*, she says. It's nerves. But Mama still won't move, won't get out of bed. The doctor arrives with stethoscope and a worn leather case full of shiny metal instruments, boxes of pills, and mysterious potions. Mama has had a nervous breakdown; that's what the doctor calls it. Is there any reason Doña Emily might have had an attack of the nerves? No, not really, Daddy says. She never gets sick. I bite my tongue until it bleeds. *No reason? No reason?*

The doctor shakes his head and says she needs to get to the *clínica* in El Seybo. "There's something wrong, but I can't really help her. But they have doctors with more training there—even doctors for the head." He means the mind, I know. I've read about psychiatrists, but they're for people who go crazy. "I've given her a *calmante* for her nerves," he says. "But she should go as soon as possible. Today. I'll see if Padre Daniel can take her in his jeep."

Livia gets Mama to sit up. She looks at Daddy finally. Her eyes are glazed, but at least she's talking now. "They want to take me to El Seybo? No, no. I'm fine, really. Just tired." She closes her eyes as if she's going to lie back down in bed, but the nurse props her up like a doll and begins to remove her nightgown. I watch from the doorway. I'm not used to seeing Mama naked. Her breasts droop against her chest as she steps into her underwear. She sits listlessly as Livia lifts her arms and slips the brassiere straps over them. I move past her to Mama's small closet and select her travel dress, the light blue one that doesn't wrinkle in long car rides. I stare at the sight of my mother unable to help herself. Fingers of fear push into my throat and I feel like I'm going to throw up. But I shake it off. Mama sees me then. I can tell she recognizes me, but her eyes are all soft and unfocused from the *calmante*.

"The doctor," she shrugs, "thinks I must to go to the *clínica* in El Seybo. Oh, well, have to obey doctor's orders, I guess," as if she's just humoring him. I nod, straightening up, so she doesn't see how scared I am.

Padre Daniel and his Jeep carry Mama over the mountain to the clinic in El Seybo. The nurse's sister Amelia comes twice a day and brings food we can heat up for lunch and dinner. It tastes much better than Mama's cooking, which is bland. I know I shouldn't think that. I do my lessons every day, and Daisy and Zuleica come to play most afternoons. At sunset Daddy pulls out the Scrabble game and we sit on the porch and play a game. He fixes himself a drink but only has one before dinner. I'm not used to being with Daddy alone, and I think it's strange for him too. We don't talk much, but we play our word games in some kind of truce. I beat him sometimes and he says "good going." I show him one of my paintings that I've been working on, and he tells me the perspective is slightly off. He pulls out a piece of paper and shows me where to position the vanishing point in a picture so that it reads true. I heat up Amelia's stewed chicken and set the table.

Daddy settles into reading after his meal. After washing up, I usually read in bed, but tonight I bring my drawing tablet out and sit near him in the living room. He looks at me in surprise and then goes back to his *National Geographic*. I'll get to read it when he's done.

Daddy goes up to Cocoloco for two days to tend to the copra. Amelia stays with me while he's gone, sleeping in Berta's bed. I wake in the middle of the night and for a moment think it's Berta softly snoring. Then I grip my stomach, nauseous. *Can't think about Berta being dead.* She can't be. I reach out and find Bobby sleeping by my feet, and pull his warm body up next to me. He squirms, then sighs and settles in. He seems to know I'm upset, and I place my hand against his little chest as he breathes. In and out, in and out. As if there's nothing wrong; as if it's that easy to fall back to sleep. The worst part is when I wake up and the dread flows in. Like a liquid seeping through all my veins, a poison spreads until my whole body is a mass of fear, a dark swamp like the bottom of the *laguna*, where everything is dangerous.

On a rainy morning Padre Daniel takes Daddy to pick up Mama from the clinic. Amelia cleans the house and I fidget and pace, waiting for them to come home. The rain worsens and the bay is lit with lightning and thunder. I worry about the mountain road, which can wash out in storms. The rain pounds onto the aluminum roof, and it fills the house with noise, so I don't hear the bell when the back gate opens. Suddenly Mama and Daddy are home. She looks pale and weak, but her eyes are clear as she leans to give me a squeeze. Daddy lights a cigarette and reaches out with a hand to my shoulder to join in the hug. I hesitate between wanting to shrug him away, as if I didn't see his gesture, and wanting to pull him close.

Daddy stays sober as Mama recovers. She goes back to her old routines as if nothing out of the ordinary has taken place. Sometimes I catch her just gazing off to the horizon, but she doesn't seem to be looking at anything in particular. At the end of the day, they nurse their five o'clock drinks and resume their sunset-watching hour on the pier. I begin to breathe more easily. Our nights now are like a pot that's been turned down to simmer after it boiled over and made a mess of the entire stove —the kind that you scrub and scrub but there's always a patch of burnt residue that won't go away. I slide into the background again. I figure it's just a matter of time before the pot starts to heat up again. But for a long time Daddy stays relatively sober, working harder and longer days.

Berta's absence keeps me silent company, filling my dreams with sadness. We never talk, any of us, about her during this time. I walk the empty beach with Bobby and think of all the times Berta and I hiked the shore, looking for shells, and how she'd jump into the bay and swim parallel to the surf as fast as she could until she got out of breath. Bobby would follow her into the waves but couldn't keep up with her. He'd turn around and paddle ashore, barking at her until he got distracted by a scuttling crab. I splashed in the shallows; I was afraid of the deep water because I couldn't see below the surface without my glasses. After her swim, Berta would throw herself on the sand, panting from the effort. Bobby would run back and jump on her and we'd all roll around in the waves, sandy and salty, and Berta would snort with laughter.

I find Mama, one morning in June, emptying Berta's dresser. Wordlessly, she gives me some shirts and a skirt I've suddenly grown into. What doesn't fit me she folds and puts in a cardboard box. Will they show up on one of the village orphans, or will she just throw it all away? The questions lurk in the corners like ghosts, faintly visible but never acknowledged. Will we ever speak the truth—and if we do, will Berta's memory disappear like a passing storm? It never seems odd to me that we don't have any kind of private funeral or memorial service, or do anything at all that relates to the yellowing newspaper clipping tucked away in Mama's jewelry box, underneath Berta's last letter.

Chapter Seventeen

❄

Bobby

Mama and Daddy are trying extra hard to save money since I'll be going to boarding school next year for tenth grade. With the instability in the government, the price for copra has plunged again. Daddy has to sell more copra to make up for the loss of income, and he's working almost twice as many hours as usual. At least that means he doesn't drink quite as much, so our nights are sometimes peaceful.

I begin to paint self-portraits, which I keep hidden under the bed. In them, I'm peering from behind a wall, and only part of me shows—one eye, part of a nose and mouth. I can't seem to imagine what being whole looks like, much less feels like. I get quiet inside when I'm working on a picture, and I'm not aware that hours have passed. It's like when I read a good book and all of a sudden it's suppertime and I haven't noticed it's getting dark outside. Painting is when my mind goes blank except for what's right in front of me. I forget about Daddy's last episode, or stop thinking about Berta. When I'm tired of self-portraits, I decide I'll draw Bobby. He mostly just lies around these days, which makes it easy to work on my picture. He's ten now, which I guess is pretty old in dog years, but I'm getting worried about him. He's too listless. I pick him up and he whines like he is in pain. I get hot all over and begin to shiver. I swallow hard.

"Mama, something's wrong with Bobby."

She frowns. "He hasn't been himself lately, has he? Maybe he got into some stickers." She crouches down and pats him on the head. He licks her hand and wags his tail, but it's a slow wag, and then he tucks his tail between his legs again.

"Let's look at you," Mama says. She runs her fingers over his legs and paws. "Nothing wrong here." Bobby rolls over and Mama pats at his belly, which looks a little swollen. He whimpers and I catch my breath.

Daddy examines him next and clicks his tongue. "He's got some kind of lump." He pokes around some more and Bobby gives a sharp yelp.

"Can we get a doctor to fix it?" My voice quavers. "Please?"

Mama bicycles to the *clínica* later that day and talks with an *enfermera*, a nurse. The doctor is away for a few days, but she'll tell him to come see us when he's back. He shows up the next week and shakes his head as he inspects Bobby. "*Lo siento*," he says. "I'm sorry." It's a tumor and there's nothing he can do. It will only get worse. He can come back and give him some kind of shot, if we want to put him out of his pain that way.

I start shaking and can't stop. Why didn't I notice this

before? Maybe we could have fixed him up if I'd paid more attention. I guess I just took him for granted—my little wiggling dog, happy to walk the *finca* trails with Daddy, or beg for meat scraps from Mama, or patiently sit for me to remove ticks. Daddy has always been gentle with Bobby and never yells at him. If I want to think any good thoughts about Daddy, I just imagine him sitting in his chair after lunch, reading a book while Bobby snoozes in his lap. Sometimes Daddy falls asleep too. When he gets up he says they both needed their siestas. It's as if Daddy softens up around Bobby; our dog is the only member of our family that we can all love all the time. He gets the hugs and pats I rarely experience, but I don't mind that because he is such a good dog.

Daddy says, "We'll take care of Bobby." His eyes are red too. Mama thanks the doctor, wiping tears from her eyes. The next day Pedro, one of Daddy's workers, comes by the house, his machete, as always, dangling in a sheath from his belt. Daddy and he walk out to the pier to talk. At first I think the man is here on *finca* business. I rub Bobby behind his ears, which usually elicits little "woofs" of pleasure. He wags his tail, and my eyes sting with tears. "I love you," I whisper. "I love you. We'll make you better. You'll see." I don't believe my own words but I say them anyway, over and over. Then Daddy and Pedro walk back into the house.

"It's time to say good-bye to Bobby." Mama's tone is soft and sad. I don't have to ask what's going to happen. I try not to look at the machete, so sharp it can slice through a coconut in one blow. I hold Bobby one last time. His eyes are bright, and he tries to lick the salt tears from my face. I can't say good-bye. I can only whimper and touch his fur very gently, so it doesn't hurt him. My heart is thumping and I think I'll break apart. *No, no, no!* I scream inside and then I'm wailing out loud, harder even than when I cried for Berta, and I don't care, I don't try to hold anything inside. I realize I'm screaming when I see Bobby looking at me, startled, and I stop. *Don't scare Bobby*, I think. I grab Mama's hand and she holds it tightly. Daddy now has his arm around Mama and pulls me to him. He's shaking too. I can hardly breathe.

For a while we just stand there, as if we can stop what is coming, then Pedro finally clears his throat and gets down on his knees. He cradles Bobby in a towel, his cracked brown fingers holding him like a baby in its blanket. Bobby doesn't resist. Mama and Daddy walk with him as far as the beach path, then turn back, holding hands. Daddy wipes his eyes and blows his nose. The worker walks out of sight, headed towards the mouth of the Yeguada, where the current flows swiftly out into the bay. I run to my room and shut the curtain. I don't want to see him returning, empty-handed, the belt with its hanging knife wiped clean by river water.

I DRIFT THROUGH THE DAYS in a gray haze, doing my schoolwork, walking the four kilometers to Cocoloco every few days with Mama as Daddy buries himself in work at the *finca*. Now I can see the pain in Mama's eyes and in Daddy's downturned mouth. It's like we couldn't or wouldn't mourn for Berta, but the shock of Bobby's loss is so great it has awakened a mountain of grief in all of us. It's too big to talk about, but somehow it's made Daddy slow down his drinking. I can see him trying to curb his temper by taking more long swims at the end of the day instead of long swigs of rum. Sometime Mama strokes my head when I'm near, like she used to pat Bobby. But we still have to keep up the fake stories to everyone in town. I'm getting better now at answering questions about Berta. My lies slip out automatically, like a song I know the words to by heart. But the toothaches I used to get when I was younger have come back, and I catch the *gripe* twice in three months. I have a low constant pain in my gut, especially at night when I cradle a pillow and moan—silently, so as not to wake anyone up. I dream Bobby is snoring next to me with his paws clawing my arms, but it's my own fingers digging and I wake up with scratch marks and a cloud of dread.

I want a storm to come and destroy everything, to tear the house apart and sweep me out to sea in a tidal wave. I think I'll get my wish when a hurricane lashes us at the end of summer, whipping up the harbor like egg whites. Winds churn the palm fronds into a fever and waves thunder all day and night. Trembling clouds of spume fly through the air, coating fences and houses and leaving lacy ghosts that dry up and disappear. I stand in the stinging rain, mouth open to receive its punishment. But of course Casalata survives the hurricane. When we hear it has reached Florida, the eye a hundred miles across, I wish I could be worrying about Berta—as if she's still living there, as if she's still living.

Instead, I try to stow away my feelings, those thoughts that want me to drown in the ocean or a storm or get hit by lightning—or to hit something really hard. I don't dare think about what or whom I'd want to hit—just that I want to hurt something. But those are bad thoughts, so I stuff them inside until they're just a block of hardness behind my belly.

Hermanas Mirabel

Chapter Eighteen

⁂

Butterflies and Ambushes

In the daytime I immerse myself in the local paper. Trujillo's generosity to the hurricane victims makes the headlines. There is other news, too, of suspected plots against *El Jefe*. The plotters are named and jailed swiftly, the editorials report. I'm pulled in by a story of a car accident involving three sisters whose pictures I've seen before in the paper. Four young women—the Mirabal sisters—were once part of Ciudad Trujillo's elite, but now are enemies of the state. Several of them have been jailed before because their husbands are accused of plotting against Trujillo. The sisters are referred to as *Las Mariposas*—The Butterflies— and yesterday three of them died in an automobile accident on a mountain road. The paper shows a photograph of their jeep after it crashed to the bottom of a cliff. It looks like a crushed insect, wheels upturned and doors splayed open like broken wings. The report says the sisters were on their way to the prison where their husbands were incarcerated because *El Jefe*, in his goodness, had granted them permission to visit their spouses in prison.

When Daddy reads the story, he mutters to Mama that this was no accident. One of their friends says he heard the sisters were dead before the vehicle tumbled over the cliff—that they were waylaid on the mountain road and strangled. The victims were shoved back in their jeep and it was pushed off the cliff. The next week this is confirmed by the newspaper. Now Trujillo makes frequent public speeches about how a special team is investigating this awful crime against these poor, helpless "*Mariposas.*"

In Miches, people whisper that Trujillo himself ordered the assassination. The *Mariposas* are now on everyone's lips. Three women have been murdered, but they've unleashed thousands of rumors that flit like butterflies all across the countryside. The murmurings grow louder every day, as if a hurricane of gossip is circling this island and it's not going to blow away any time soon.

The story makes me think of Berta. Was she murdered? She wasn't anyone's enemy. She was just my sister. "Was," I say to myself. I don't know, I tell myself. Maybe she's still alive. Maybe it's someone else that washed ashore like a piece of driftwood. No, don't think that either. If she is alive, why doesn't she write? *Stop thinking.* I try to forget about the butterflies in my stomach and the ones flying through the air around us.

I distract myself by reading the latest US magazines that the Breedens send us, *Newsweek* and *Time.* The articles about the Dominican Republic are completely different than anything written in *El Caribe*. I feel like I'm reading something dangerous, forbidden.

Daddy is working at the *finca* this week, so Mama and I trudge up to Cocoloco to bring him supplies and spend the night. I'm drifting off to sleep when voices in English break the quiet. From the direction of the beach we hear loud yells: "Yoo-hoo, Jesse? Emily? Surprise!"

Flashlight beams flicker in our general direction, like large fireflies, as the night visitors find the path to the house. Shouldering knapsacks, two figures emerge into the circle of lamplight, shaking off sand and saltwater. It's the Breedens.

"Bet you're shocked to see us!" Norma cackles, catching her breath at the same time. "We wrote you a couple of weeks ago that we'd be coming. Guess you didn't get it. Anyway, when we got to Miches and saw Casalata all closed up, we figured oh hell, we can make it up the damn beach to Cocoloco before dark."

Ed eases the pack off and rolls his eyes. "We were dead wrong." Norma shakes her wet hair like a dog. "And I fell in both rivers—but hey, we made it!" They seem awfully cheerful about their ordeal, and then I see the half-empty vodka bottle Norma is waving as she talks. Mama brings towels and finds them dry clothes. We all sit at the picnic table downstairs while Mama puts leftover spaghetti in a pan to heat on the Coleman stove. The Breedens know about Berta, so that's a relief. No lies needed here. Norma gives me a vodka kiss and Ed offers me a damp hug. He reminds me of an old dog with his wobbly jowl and sad, droopy eyes. Norma is thin, like one of those skinny greyhounds, all nervous energy and sharp teeth. I think that I'd like Ed as a father; he's kind and talks to me like I'm worth listening to.

"Hoo-boy, things are bad in the capital," Ed says as he towels off his hair. He says the US has severed diplomatic relations with the Dominican Republic and sent the ambassador packing. He hands the towel to Mama and sits down heavily.

"The CIA has taken over the American Consulate in Ciudad Trujillo."

Norma interrupts. "Hell yes, and the secret police are everywhere. Was it last week, Ed, when they killed four people on Avenida Gomez?"

Ed nods. That's the street in the capital where most of the foreign embassies have their offices. "The Goat denies it"— that's what they call Trujillo—"but it's true. He says everything's under control. Of course you've heard about the Mirabal girls?" He shakes his head. "I'm guessing something big is up, and it will affect all of us."

I shiver a little. Norma leans forward and stabs her cigarette in the air like a weapon. "I'd sure get out if we goddamn could." She emphasizes the "goddamn" and glares at Ed briefly, then smiles. "But I guess we're all in it for the long haul. What the hell, let's have another drink."

Ed looks at her and says, "Now, honey, don't get started."

Mama says let's forget about politics now and the Breedens finish their meal. Daddy brings the old Victrola down from upstairs and cranks it up. I climb the stairs to the crooning of Frank Sinatra. Eventually everyone else stumbles up to sleep. I dream of butterflies and spiderwebs and cars smashed like insects.

The next day we all hike back to Miches. I'm sent to sleep over at my friend Daisy's house so Ed and Norma can have my bedroom in Casalata. Daisy lives in a small wooden house with a porch and outside kitchen. The wallboards are warped and let slivers of light in from the street. We share a bed under a drooping mosquito net. We giggle at her mother's snores in the other room and stay up late looking at American fashion magazines. After she switches off the light, Daisy wraps her arm around me and we nestle together like two spoons in a kitchen drawer. I find tears spilling out of my eyes and wonder why, until I remember that the only people who hug me are Dominicans. Daddy used to, when I was really little and he liked to hold me in his lap. He still kisses me goodnight, but his lips are big and wet and smell like cigarettes or rum or both. It makes me sick. Mama gives me dry little kisses at bedtime— reminding me of bird pecks. I can't remember her arms around me, ever, at all. I stare at the patterns of the streetlight coming through the cracks until I fall asleep.

For my fifteenth birthday Mama lets me have a party, and Daddy says I'm old enough to have beer if I want to. My parents will go to the Candelarios' house for dinner so we kids are alone. Daddy's left one bottle of Bermudez rum on the kitchen counter for the older boys, but I hide it in a cupboard when he's not looking. There's a light shower just after dusk. The rain brings out the *macos*, black frogs that climb out of the *laguna* to feed on insects along the path. I pick them up, one at a time, and fling them out of the way. Daisy's aunt Rebeca will come with the rest of the girls as chaperone, but she's just nineteen and likes to dance, so we don't mind.

I hold the glass of beer carefully so I don't ruin my new dress, which everyone says makes me look *muy señorita*, very grown-up. The beer is cold and I drink it all down right away. It makes me dizzy; I fumble over to the edge of the *laguna* and throw up. Across the pond a frog croaks and a small silver fish jumps out of the water, making the surface flutter in the moonlight. I slink back inside to sponge off my soiled dress and brush my teeth. *Stupid*, I say to the mirror. Zuleica's boyfriend Bienve pulls me aside after I join the group. He says he'd just gone to pee over in the bushes, and he heard a noise at the other side of the fence. There are men over there.

"They're watching the house. I think they're *cascas blancas*—I could see the helmet on one of them."

"No!" He must be joking. The *cascas blancas* are some sort of special government forces who spy on people. I've read about them in the paper, but there can't possibly be any of those in Miches.

"*Ven, ven*," he whispers. Come, come, I'll show you. We peer through a hole in the shrubbery and see lumpy shapes, four or five men, all lined up in a row. Maybe it's the lingering effect of the beer, but it occurs to me how little I know about this country. How many nights have we been spied upon? I don't worry that anyone will think Daddy is a *Yanqui imperialista* or that our family is in any kind of danger. We've been here too long, and Daddy's reputation—embarrassing as it is—stretches far beyond Miches. We learned once from a stranger in San Pedro, clear on the other side of the country, that yes, they knew about the *Americano loco* in Miches, with his little metal house and a farm he named Cocoloco.

Someone must have sent spies to make sure my friends aren't turning into hidden revolutionaries. That makes no sense, either. I'm lost in thought when Bienve tugs at my hand and we back out of the bushes quietly. Word gets around to all but the party proceeds as if everything is normal. Which I guess it is, really. Matilde switches off the lights and Bienve stops a record in mid-play as everyone sings "*Feliz cumpleaños*"—Happy birthday. I close my eyes and take a big breath and I wish the spies away; I wish Daddy will stop drinking; I wish Berta were alive and here; then I blow out the candles.

I wait until breakfast to tell Mama and Daddy about the strangers in the bushes. Daddy puts down his coffee cup with a frown. "Well, I guess it isn't that surprising," he says. "It must be outsiders. But, Chrissakes, why now? Like *we* have state secrets? Oh, well, another reason to keep our lips zipped." Mama nods her head and takes a long drag from her cigarette, her eyes gazing at some far off point on the horizon.

THE BREEDEN'S PREDICTION that "something big" is going to happen finally comes true when His Excellency Generalísimo Rafael Molinas Trujillo, the Supreme Benefactor, *El Líder*, *El Jefe*, is assassinated. On his way to visit a favorite mistress outside of Ciudad Trujillo, his motorcade is ambushed by a group of men who have been planning his killing for a long time. We first hear the news when one of Daddy's workers comes running to our back gate, ringing the bell over and over and shouting.

"Goodness," Mama says at the clamor, opening the front door. It is still early morning, much too soon for *finca* business or even the milk vendors. Daddy is in the bathroom shaving and I'm still in bed.

When she comes back, her face is gray. "Trujillo's dead." Daddy whistles, low, and plugs in the portable radio. A solemn newsman on Radio Caribe is lamenting the inconceivable loss of the supreme leader, brought down by scum, by cowards. Then we hear "CIA," and they're saying it's a plot from the *Yanqui imperialistas*. Another reporter says there are many rumors that it isn't even true—there's been no assassination at all. It might just be a plot to see who his traitors are. *El Jefe* is really still alive and he's sailed to Puerto Rico on the presidential yacht, *Angelina*. It's a cruel joke—it has to be—but finally the assassination is confirmed. No one says a word against *El Jefe*— not out loud, anyway, and not for a long time. Daddy says we'll ride this storm out just fine. He says things will actually improve in time. "We'll just sit tight, although it's going to be a bouncy ride."

What does he think we're on, a roller coaster? I know all about their surviving the great hurricane of 1938 in New England. I know Daddy froze almost to death on an engineering assignment in Russia one winter before the war. So I guess I can understand why we'll stay put—this is just another crisis that will go away. As we wait for news of who's going to run the country, we hear the US is sending ships and troops to protect American interests in the republic. Daddy says President Kennedy is just trying to be sure no Commies try to take over, like Castro did in Cuba. We don't need help anyway, he says; we just have to keep making copra. Joaquín Balaguer is installed as President, and he manages to withstand the Trujillo family's attempts at taking over. Former Trujillo mourners topple monuments and statues of *El Jefe* throughout the country. The capital's name is changed from Ciudad Trujillo to its former name, Santo Domingo. I stop trying to understand what's happening; it's all very confusing. Daddy is right. Life does continue much the same as always. I guess we're too far from all the action here in our faraway village.

We stay away from the capital because there it's different. Anti-American sentiment is growing larger every day, like a thundercloud building off on the horizon. In Miches, people say bad things about the *Yanquis*, but since we've been part of this community for over a decade already we know they don't mean us. Daddy isn't drinking as much as he used to, although he still flares up every now and then. I tell myself it's only one more year before I get to escape to Florida and a new life. But now I dread it as much as I long for it. Berta won't be there waiting for me. No one will be.

Chapter Nineteen

米

American Dream

The mail comes with a brochure from a boarding school in central Florida. It shows buildings surrounded by pine and oak trees trailing lacy Spanish moss from their branches. A pretty blonde girl poses by the front portico, smiling up at a boy holding a book. The school is just outside the town of Howey-in-the-Hills, which I imagine as having steep winding streets and picturesque shops just like a *Saturday Evening Post* cover by Norman Rockwell.

I used to think I'd be sent to an American school in the capital after my correspondence courses ended, but Mama says it's too unstable in Santo Domingo these days and I might not be safe. It's been over a year since Trujillo's assassination, but the new government is shaky. I decide not to think about that; I worry instead about how I'm going to look when I get to Florida and whether there will be a tall boy to dance with when I get to the coed school.

I look at my clothing: homemade shorts and stained shirts and the two dresses that still fit me, one of them clearly showing Mama's careful mending after I snagged it on a thorn bush. The town seamstress stitches me up two skirts, one that will also go with a new store-bought sweater. Jittery with excitement, I pack a month before I'm going to leave. And just like that, I'm finally on my way. At the airport, Daddy crushes me in a squeeze. I see he's crying but making no noise. I look away as he blows his nose and tries to wink at me.

"See you later, alligator." We heard that on a rock and roll record last summer, and it's now Daddy's standard good-bye.

"After awhile, crocodile," I answer, choked up too. I hug him back, not minding his sweat-stained shirt. He looks lost all of a sudden, not scary at all. I cling to Mama, afraid to leave her smell, her skin. Her blue eyes are full of tears and sadness but she smiles anyway.

THE NEXT DAY I'M ON A BUS heading for a brand new life. It turns out there are no hills to speak of in Florida. For mile after mile I stare out the bus window as flatness drones by, horizontal lines punctured occasionally by perpendicular roads. Alongside the highway, pines and palmettos stand at attention. Houses are single-story, sprawling rectangles that all look the same. As we motor up the coast, the Atlantic sparkles on the right. Even the royal palms grow straight up, as if that is the rule here. In the Dominican Republic the land curves up into mountains, slides down into ragged bays and undulating meadows. Roads slither like snakes, and even some hovels are decorated with trills of curving iron railings. Florida looks more like a geometry lesson.

Finally the bus heads inland, the angularity now broken by swamps and rivers. The air is softer here, but also heavy. I'm wearing the sweater set, which is much too hot, and a new pair of shoes I haven't broken in yet, so I have blisters on both ankles. In the seat in front of me, a small child whimpers and his mother fans him with a magazine. I try not to think of Berta, of baby Mitch, but I can't help it. What would he look like now? Could he be this child—this very one?

Shut up, I tell myself—*just stop thinking.*

Howey-in-the-Hills doesn't exactly live up to its name; it has no steep winding streets or real hills at all, just some hillocks near a lake. The air is humid and hot, no tropic breezes to cool my anxiety. Live oak trees with twisted branches hang heavy with Spanish moss. I feel all out of place. My hair is all wrong, the pleats in my skirt too wide and the pattern too bright. The other girls giggle and float in dainty dresses with subtle floral patterns—Villagers, I'm sure. According to *Seventeen Magazine*, Villager is the favorite clothing brand of discerning teenagers everywhere. Boys mill around the girls like bees. I feel lightheaded. Everybody else looks like they belong in this picture, and it's not a photo in *Seventeen*; this is real. My head clouds up. No one is noticing me. I'm going to be nobody here, nobody at all. In Miches, Berta and I were sought after just because we were foreigners, *extranjeros*, who lived by different rules than Dominicans. We were always going to be different. Not better than, Mama warned. Still—we could leave the country when we pleased, unlike Dominicans. And now I'm nothing special at all.

The air fills up with confusion as we sort out what line to stand in for registration and how to sign in for our dorm room.

I feel all alone in the auditorium, even though we're crammed together for the orientation session. In a daze, I notice the slicked-back hair of the boy in front of me. An older girl, maybe a senior, slouches in the seat next to me, chewing gum and applying lipstick at the same time. Her charm bracelet jangles as she catches me staring, and she frowns slightly then yawns, as if this is all very boring—as if I'm boring too.

I wonder if it was this way for Berta. Was she also scared? I can't help thinking about her now, even though I try to push any thoughts about her away because I don't want to cry. I finally get to move into the dorm room I'll share with Beth Porter for the next year. I know her name from the dorm sign-up list. The door is open and I see two beds are perpendicular to each other. A tall girl with brown hair waves me in.

"Hi, I'm Beth." She gestures to the closet. "Let me know if you need more space." I lug my one suitcase onto the bed and when I'm done unpacking, she says, "Is that all you have?" Then she makes a face and says, "I'm sorry, I didn't mean how that came out."

"It's okay," I say. I don't know what to say to her, but that's not a problem. Beth likes to talk. She tells me right away about her boyfriend Charlie. Beth says she is at the boarding school because she goofed off in ninth grade in public school and her parents thought private school would help.

"Are your parents very mad at you?" I ask, puzzled by her cheerful tone when it sounds to me like she's been sent here as punishment. Berta and I didn't dare get bad grades at home. That would risk a beating with Daddy's old leather belt.

"Mad?" she asks, shaking her head no. "They just want to get me away from Charlie so I can concentrate on my studies. Not that they don't like him—they do."

"So you're not afraid of your father?"

Beth looks at me and furrows her brow. "Scared of Dad? Nah. I guess Mom's the tough one, but she's okay too. She nags a lot, though. I won't miss that."

I sit back against the pillows and try to imagine what it would be like to be in a family like this, to be unafraid of my father—to like him, even.

"So you know all about me," Beth says. "Okay, your turn."

I start to tell her about Miches, about Casalata and Cocoloco, and as I'm talking, these names sound peculiar and silly all of a sudden. She asks about my family. I look down at the pillowcase I'm twisting into a knot and say something safe, like Mama likes to read books and that Daddy was an engineer before he became a coconut farmer. I describe the *finca* and how pretty the beach is.

"Do you have any sisters or brothers?"

I stop. Do I? Did I? I stutter and say no, just me. I get up quickly, saying I have to use the bathroom. To my relief, she returns to the subject of Charlie, and then the lunch bell rings and we head off together to the adventure of our first meal in the school cafeteria.

Two of my teachers stop by my desk after classes and ask, "Didn't your sister used to attend here? What happened to her? She was such a good student. Is she in college now?" To them I just nod, yes, yes, she's fine. Luckily Beth isn't in either of those classes, but it's getting hard to keep straight what I've told to whom.

I get in trouble the second week of school at evening study hall. Beth and I have both finished our homework, so I start drawing, copying a picture from an art book. It's Botticelli's Venus painting, and I exaggerate her bare breasts and flying snake hair and the clamshell at her feet. When I finish, I pass it to Beth. I don't notice the study hall monitor has been watching the exchange. I'm washing my hair in the sink that night after dinner when a loud rap on the door interrupts the quiet. Mrs. Hitchens, the housemother, is standing outside. She's built like a fireplug, with badly dyed red hair and bow legs. She points at me and says the dean wants to see me, right now, in his office. I have no idea why, and my hair is full of shampoo. "Rinse it out," she barks. "He's waiting." I slip on shorts and a sweatshirt and wrap my dripping head in a towel.

The dean is frowning under the glare of a desk lamp. He picks up a crumpled piece of paper and shoves the Venus drawing at me. I stare back, afraid. "I know this is yours, young lady. I can have you expelled. Do you want to go home; is that it?"

"No, no. It was just a joke," I stammer. I can't continue; my throat has tightened up. I squirm in the chair. I can't go home— Daddy will disown me too, and then what will happen? The clock behind the desk ticks, ticks, ticks. I strangle a cough. The dean finally pulls the paper back and rips it up. "Consider this a warning."

Beth is in bed, looking at a magazine, when I come in and burst out crying. She puts her arm around my shoulder as I tell her what happened. "Don't worry," she says. "Hey, your drawing was good—he wouldn't know real art if he saw it." I feel comforted by Beth's words. She acts as if I need taking care of, or at least watching over. It's a really odd feeling—that someone wants to protect me. As the days go by, Beth says she feels sorry for what she calls my "sheltered life" and shows me how to apply makeup correctly and how to use curlers to get the most lift for my limp hair.

At least here I know exactly where I'm supposed to be and what I'm supposed to do. At night I don't have too many nightmares, and there aren't any crickets to hunt down and kill. On Sundays we wear our school blazers and attend chapel. It's the first time I've sat through any religious service. Mr. McFarland is the chaplain and school counselor. He's a thin man with dark hair and brown eyes, and he wears horn-rimmed glasses. I ask Beth what a counselor does, and she says he helps kids who are in trouble. I like sitting in the darkened chapel as his calm voice leads us in prayer or song. I can't imagine why Daddy would think this kind of thing is so terrible. Mr. McFarland's sermons are about forgiveness and caring, and I drink up all the words like I've been dying of thirst and didn't know it until now. After chapel, he usually waits at the doorway and greets students who want to talk. I want to meet him, but I feel shy and awkward, so I just rush out as if I can't wait to get in line for lunch.

I get almost used to the food here. The cafeteria serves up big flat hamburgers, greasy hot dogs, runny mashed potatoes, and canned vegetables and fruit. No fresh avocados, mangos, or pineapple so tangy it makes your mouth water just thinking about it. Here we get Jell-O for dessert, or bread pudding, which Beth says they make from old, stale slices left over from breakfast.

On a Saturday, Beth and I take a bus to a nearby town to stock up on makeup at the Eckerds Drugstore. This seems unnecessary to me because Beth's shelf by the sink already overflows with jars and tubes of everything from hairspray to face cream. Beth picks up a wire basket and strides right through the chaos of products to the Maybelline counter, where she's going to buy the latest color, "Tangerine Kiss." I figure her allowance must be bigger than mine, but then she shows me the bargain bin, where she says we can get really good stuff for almost nothing. I poke around, lost, and she says no, not that brand, it's not good—but here, this is great. I end up with a new lipstick and brown eyeliner Beth says will make my eyes stand out, which I learn is very important since I wear glasses.

We walk past the window of Howey Homes, Inc. with their big sign boasting Beautiful Home Sites on Little Lake Harris, and peer in at the women getting their hair done at the Pleeze-U Beauty Salon. The hamburger place is full of students, but now that I've had an education in makeup buying, I feel almost like one of them now, not just an odd girl from a foreign country. We order fountain Cokes and moon pies, which are big cookies with white marshmallowy stuff smashed between them.

Every day feels a little safer, especially at night after lights out. It's the first time I haven't had to fear the sound of Daddy's voice raised in a drunken muddle. Here the nights cool down as fall comes on, another new sensation. I miss Mama and the ocean and the loudness of rain. Here the thunderstorms are muffled by thick walls and insulated ceilings.

Berta stays in my mind every day. I can't help but think, She was *here;* she was in this dorm, maybe even this room. She went to this class, had this teacher. To forestall questions from staff and teachers, I decide to remain invisible. This isn't hard; I've been practicing for years. No one chooses me for Phys Ed teams until there's just two or three of us still standing, the leftovers. I'm also the last pick for a biology partner. The dead frogs all splayed out in formaldehyde make me sick. At least I'm good at English and art and especially geography—from all those years of poring over every word, picture, and map in the *National Geographic*s. When grades are posted in the main building for all to see, I'm shocked to see my name on the list of students with the highest grades. I hear "Good going," and there's the dean standing behind me, his eyes no longer stern. As he smiles, I wonder if he's noticed I got an A+ in art.

One Sunday I finally linger after chapel to meet Mr. McFarland. I tell him my name and how much I like his sermons, but he looks at me oddly like we've already met, and then asks if I'm related to Berta Gardner, who was here a few years ago. I look around to see if anyone else is listening, but no one is in earshot. I can't pretend I didn't hear his question, nor can I run away, because he's still holding my hand in his. His eyes see all the way to the places I keep hidden, where the secrets live. I can't speak, but I start to shudder.

Mr. McFarland pulls me quickly into his office and closes the door. He motions to a chair and I fall into it, my throat tight, swollen shut. "There, there," he says, and that remark sounds oddly funny to me, and I snort, half laughing and half crying. He pulls out a white handkerchief that smells like Ivory soap. "Here," he says, and I'm embarrassed that I'm laughing, because nothing is funny. I've read about people getting all hysterical. That's it. I'm hysterical and insane. I want to leave the room, but I can't move. Mr. McFarland just sits there. I mush up the handkerchief and wipe my face until the cloth is damp with tears. "I'm sorry," I say to the soiled handkerchief, as if I've done it some wrong, and then I look at Mr. McFarland and his eyes say yes, you can say anything, everything.

And so I do. He's the first adult I've really just talked to, just straight across, no hiding, no pretending. My voice is small and tight, as if I'm squeezing out of a dark cave into sunlight and I'm not sure there isn't danger outside in all that brightness. I tell him about Daddy and how we're supposed to be a happy family but we're not. Then I stutter at the part about how Berta disappeared, and about the newspaper clipping, the one about the blonde girl found dead soon after Berta was missing, and that the girl is probably her.

Mr. McFarland asks how I felt when it all happened, and I don't know how to answer him, so I just shrug. Feel? I don't think I was allowed to feel anything. He shakes his head like he can't be hearing me right when I tell him Mama and Daddy made us keep all this terrible news our family secret. I try to explain why it's like Berta never existed at home, inside our four walls, that she's just a story we tell to other people—you know, the made-up one. I tell him I thought coming to the States would be the end of lying, at least here. But it's not. Even here, even him—there's always someone just being polite and asking the usual "tell me about your family" questions. I'm sick of telling them I'm an only child because inside my voice shouts "LIAR!"

Then I tell him that when I see any small child now, I find myself wondering, *Could this be Berta's baby boy?* As if somehow I'd know him if I saw him. Finally, there's no more to say. There's nowhere to hide now. Mr. McFarland's voice breaks in and I start crying again, but this is more like a light sprinkle left over when a storm has just passed. Mr. McFarland's eyes are wet. He says he remembers Berta well. She was special, probably one of the smartest students in the whole school. His voice wraps around me like a warm blanket. I am startled when he says that I don't have to lie to anyone anymore. Just like that.

"But—" I start.

He continues, waving my "but" aside like an annoying mosquito. He says I can say yes, I have a sister, but she's decided to go away and not tell us where she is.

"But I think she's dead."

"I understand," he says. "So leave that part out; it won't hurt as much. Tell the truth—but you don't have to tell everything. Just stop right there. If anyone asks for more, just say you'd rather not talk about it—period."

Oh. I hadn't ever thought of that. Again he asks how I'm feeling. I don't know quite how to say it, but I'm lighter inside, as if I've cried out some of the heaviness that lives there. He pats my shoulder lightly and stands up. He says to come see him any time I need to. Any time, he repeats. Later Beth comes into our dorm room and asks what's wrong, and I tell her I was talking with Mr. McFarland. She says, "Are you okay?"

I take a breath. "Can I tell you something?"

So I tell her it wasn't true when I'd said I didn't have any brothers and sisters, and even though my voice threatens to shut down, I manage to squeak out what Mr. McFarland suggested. I hold my breath, waiting to see if my short answer will be enough for her or not. All she says is, "Oh, I'm sorry." And then, after a short silence, "I bet you miss her a lot."

Chapter Twenty

❄

Cold War and Warm Holidays

Beth and I have progressed to worrying about such things as the annoying crop of pimples we both have sprouted and the nastiness of some of the students, the ones that gather like a flock of twittering birds and ignore us as if we don't even exist. They whisper about one girl behind her back because her hair is cut short like a boy's, and one of them mocks the shy boy in history class who stutters and walks with a limp. I'm still learning how to be here, as if I'm swimming in murky water where I'm not sure where the bottom is, how far the shore, or whether sharks are circling, looking for bait. I never imagined it would be like this, the part where perfect-looking students make fun of their own classmates. In Miches, nobody did that

—not to be mean, anyway. I think about a *National Geographic* article I read once about animals in the wild and how the strong cut the weak ones out of the herd in order to survive. But we're not on some African plain with lions chasing down runty calves; we're here in America, safe and sound.

I'm assigned to be hall monitor for our floor of the girl's dorm. I walk the halls after lights out and note which rooms have light under the door frame and give the room numbers to the housemother the next day. One of the popular girls gets into trouble that way; she waits for a few days until Beth is out of our room, then barges in with one of her friends. "You bitch!" she yells, and they shove me into the closet. They lock the door somehow and slam out, and I sink to the floor, feeling like the time Berta and I got locked inside a storage box in Casalata for hours before we were rescued. Panic injects me and I begin shaking as if I'll never get out. In Miches I had Berta beside me, calming me down, but now I whimper and curl up in a ball beside the dirty laundry in the darkness. My racing heart says no one will find me. Beth does, of course. She hugs me tightly, her hair smelling like Breck shampoo and minty deodorant. I breathe again and tell her what happened.

"*They're* the bitches," she says. "Come, let's walk down to the lake so you can calm down."

I'm afraid I'll run into my tormentors, but Beth says to just ignore them. We follow the footpath along the edge of the water. A light breeze comes off the lake and whispers through the pine trees. Tree branches wave in the humid air like old ladies' arms clothed in gray-green scarves of Spanish moss. I tell the housemother I don't want to be hall monitor any more.

I don't pay much attention to the news, although there's a lot of talk these days about the cold war. The US and the Soviet

Union are in an arms race. It reminds me of roosters in the Miches cockfighting ring puffing up their tail feathers to look bigger and stronger than the opponent. At chapel on Sunday, Mr. McFarland says we must all pray for our country and our president, for Mr. Khrushchev to make the right decisions, and for Cuba, so close to us, to dismantle all those deadly weapons. But in the middle of all this, our classes go on as scheduled, except for mandatory emergency drills in the auditorium. We make nervous jokes about how all those preparations won't matter anyway if we get blasted by a nuclear bomb, and as soon as we're dismissed, we focus on the school's upcoming Halloween party.

I don't have a real costume, but with lots of eyeliner and a cheap black wig from Eckerd's, which Beth whips into a mountain of teased hair, I'm supposed to be Elizabeth Taylor. It's my first Halloween party. The gym is a forest of orange and black streamers. I ruin my makeup bobbing for apples, but two boys ask me to dance anyway. I hardly remember their faces because I'm terrified they'll find out I don't know any steps to American music. I mimic them as much as I can but am glad when the party is over and I can go to bed. I still have bad dreams about Berta, but mostly I drift away with Beth's soft snores reminding me I'm not as alone as I think.

School closes for winter break and Beth invites me to spend Christmas at her home in a small town on the Gulf Coast. The Trailways bus chugs through spotty forests and around a black swamp with water so opaque it looks like the glazed eyes of dead fish. As we get closer to the coast, the swamplands fill with mangroves, their tangled roots rising out of the water like dripping skirts. When the Gulf of Mexico comes into view I'm happy to see open water and the dark gold sun dipping down to the horizon. I've forgotten how much I miss seeing the ocean, how hungry I am to breathe salt air and watch sunrises and sunsets tint the water.

"Look, look." Beth punches me with excitement when we pull into the bus parking lot. Charlie slouches against a black convertible, looking like a poster of James Dean with his dark curly hair in a ducktail. "Isn't it pretty?" I realize she's referring to the car, which she's told me is a 1960 Buick Electra with whitewall tires. Charlie's father lets him drive it on special occasions. I can't tell if Beth is more excited to see Charlie or the convertible. She runs to him and plants a kiss right on his lips in front of everyone, something no girl in Miches would be allowed to do in public.

When we get to Beth's house, Mrs. Porter opens the front door with a hug that smells like the apple pie she's baking. I met the Porters when they came to the school at Thanksgiving. She waves us in to Beth's room, where an extra bed has been made up for me. A teddy bear perches on it with paws open in welcome. In the living room, a Christmas tree is crowded with shiny ornaments, strings of real popcorn, and silver icicles. At dinner, Mr. Porter pours iced tea; there is no liquor in sight. I start to pick up my fork, but Beth's hand is on my arm, and everyone joins hands while Mrs. Porter says grace. Then everyone except me is talking at once, laughing, and eating, and it's so strange to be sitting at dinner with a family, with no reason to be silent or afraid.

The next day Charlie takes us to a drive-in hamburger place with waitresses who roller-skate out to the cars. When we get back, he says we should double-date the next night with his friend Steve. I've never been on a real date. Steve has a sandy crew cut and greenish eyes. He's just a bit taller than me, with big shoulders. I'm tongue-tied at first, but he gives me a wide smile and then we all pile into Charlie's convertible. The Shrimp Shack is at the end of a long pier and is decorated with fishing nets and glass balls, the kind that wash ashore on the beach at Cocoloco. Charlie and Steve are on their high school football team so they talk about sports until a mountain of steamed shrimp arrives, followed by a bucket of coleslaw and hush puppies. I feel all bubbly inside.

Back at the house Steve walks me to the porch and invites me to a party the next night, Christmas Eve. I'm shocked; he didn't have to ask me out again. The next afternoon Beth coaxes my straight hair into spiky rollers and when she's all done I have a rather stiff flip, courtesy of about a gallon of hair spray. Steve shows up trailing a cloud of English Leather. He's driving his uncle's beat-up Jeep, but the inside is disinfectant clean. We rattle our way to the party and can hear The Sensations halfway down the block, blasting "Let Me In." As we walk up the driveway, Steve takes my hand like it's the most natural thing to do. When they play a slow song, he pulls me close and I let him guide me as Ray Charles sings "I Can't Stop Loving You," and I manage not to step on his feet. After the party we drive back to the Porters'. He walks me up to the porch and takes my chin in his hands. Right there, he gives me a quick kiss on the lips—just a flutter, like a butterfly landing and taking off. I take a sharp breath in as he whispers, "I had a great time. Can I call you tomorrow, you know, after the Christmas stuff is over?"

"Okay," I say and melt inside the front door. Beth is still out with Charlie, but Mrs. Porter is reading in the living room. "Nice time, dear?"

"Yes ma'am." *Oh yes,* I think—*you have no idea.* I lie back on the bed, fully dressed, and replay the kiss in my mind like a record, over and over and over. The next morning is Christmas Day. Even as I untie ribbons, inside I'm unwrapping the memory of last night's kiss and know I already have the best present ever.

That afternoon Steve calls and we make plans for a beach picnic with Beth and Charlie. We squint in the low winter sun and spread out a beach blanket, anchoring it with the cooler. I dig my bare feet into sand for the first time in months as gulls squawk and scold above the whitecaps. The boys build a fire on the beach and we roast hot dogs. Charlie and Beth gather driftwood and Steve and I hunt for shells.

"Here." He hands me a shark's tooth. "Something to remember me by."

Wrapped in a blanket, we lie on the chilly winter sand, my head on his shoulder. He smells like salt and cologne and smoke. I feel comfortable and excited all at the same time. He turns my face to his and runs his finger over my lips. I study his eyes, pale green with flecks of gold. Suddenly he kisses me, and his lips are smooth and soft. I press back and he wraps his arms around me. Now his tongue is darting between my teeth and I sit up in shock. Fear seeps in like a fog, along with a low voice saying "slut, whore," and I push Steve away abruptly. My whole body is trembling now, as if Daddy were right there on this Florida beach, spitting out nasty words. I try to shake off the feeling of dread, try to shut off Daddy's voice. Now it's Berta's voice too, an anguished wail. Steve stares at me.

"You okay?"

"Yes," I manage to respond. "It's just a little cold here." That's all I can think of to say. I can't tell him about the voices in my head. He gives me his jacket and calls out to the others that we should be going. On the last day, Steve and I go one last time to the pier and he pulls my hands into his and asks me to go steady, and I laugh because I can't believe he's asking me.

"I'll write you every week, honey," he whispers as Beth and I climb aboard the bus on New Year's Day. Honey—he called me honey. I close my eyes and taste salty kisses as the bus rumbles back to school. "You're smitten!" Beth crows. *Smitten.* I like that word.

An envelope with unfamiliar handwriting arrives the next week. I tear it open and photographs from our picnic on the beach spill out. Steve writes about how he misses me, how his jeep broke down, and ends with, *Bye. Write me. Con amor, Esteban. P.S., see, I'm learning Spanish!*

I frame the picture Steve took of me with my hair messed up from the breeze and glue the shark's tooth in the corner of the frame. In the photo I've taken my glasses off; my dreamy-eyed look is really a nearsighted blurriness. Beth and I go to her home again at Easter, but it's a brief holiday so our time with the boys is short. On our last day together, Steve and I go again to the beach and snuggle against a dune. Steve is hardly breathing now, he trembles against my skin and we lie like that, not even kissing, our faces close enough to feel each other's jagged breaths in, out, in, out. He doesn't try to French kiss me this time.

After I've returned to school, Steve writes me every week, and then there's a two-week gap. When the next letter comes, he writes how his grades are getting better, that he's buying his uncle's '57 Ford for only $400. The last paragraph starts: *Do you remember Helen, the girl I was talking to at the red light at Easter? Well, today she asked me to take her to the prom, but I told her I was going steady. She's a good friend but that's all.* He ends the letter by telling me he misses me.

Of course other girls want to date Steve. Who is Helen, anyway? I don't remember her except as a honk and hello from a blonde in a car at a stoplight. I wasn't paying attention. I don't know how to respond to his letter. The next day, John, a shy boy from my biology class, asks me to our spring dance. I don't know what to do but finally I say yes. That night I sit down to write Steve, tearing up draft after draft, until I finally write that he should go to his prom if he wants to, and that I've accepted an invitation to a dance myself—but that it's not a real date either. I don't tell him John is six foot two and nice looking in a gangly sort of way, except when he's on the basketball court, when he shoots balls into the basket like a magician. Steve writes back and says he went fishing on prom weekend, but that he might take Helen to a movie one of these days, and hopes I had fun at my dance. The last day before I leave school for the summer, I get a postcard of a Gulf Coast beach with a pier in the foreground and sand dunes off to the right, just like when we were together. In blue ink, a heart and an arrow point to one of the dunes. Steve writes: *Be a good girl and behave yourself this summer. See you later, unless either one of us begins dating someone else, ha ha! Hasta luego. Love, Esteban.*

My stomach tightens up, even though it makes sense that he'll probably begin dating. It's not like we're in the same town, and besides, we'll never be together during the summertime since that's when I go home to Miches, which is also where I'll be after I graduate. I pack the postcard in my suitcase anyway. It does say "Love," after all. Something to remember him by.

Chapter Twenty-One

✳

Miches Summer

The plane flies low over the Caribbean and circles the rocky shoreline. I strain against the cold glass as my eyes feed on the bright turquoise water with its patches of white lace where coral reefs rise up to shatter the surface. The plane dips and we surprise a field of cows when we land with a series of jolts and thumps. Passengers applaud and whistle, thanking *Dios* and the *Virgen Altagracia* for a safe landing, as if the pilot didn't have anything to do with our survival. The woman in the seat next to me packs up her rosary beads; I think she prayed all the way from Miami.

The plane door opens and thick tropical air swirls in, heavy with an aroma of hot tarmac, engine fuel, and salt breeze. I sniff the familiar scents and it's like the months in Florida never happened at all. School, Beth, even Steve seem like parts of a dream stuffed into my suitcase, packed away for now. My heart thumps and there's Daddy waving and I can't believe it but I'm glad to see him—well, just a little anyway. Clouds of cigarette smoke mingle with perfume and burned coffee from the *cafecito* stand. The line for foreigners entering the country is very short. Armed soldiers patrol the airport, toting machine guns on straps. Mama's hair is now getting white. She and Daddy strain against the metal fence that separates visitors from passengers. They both look beaten down, like prisoners. I gulp and lunge through the door to Daddy's embrace. He's all ribs and bones, his skin tobacco-brown and wrinkled. His heart is beating fast as I bury my face against his neck. Mama's hair is limp with sweat and her shoulders curve inward as if she's been holding off an enemy for a long time but has now given up the fight.

Daddy pulls back and wipes his eyes, then straightens up, taking charge. He lights a cigarette and coughs, a scraping, ugly sound. "Okay then, let's get the hell out of here."

The young guard at the gate asks for our papers. "I live here," Daddy says. The guard cocks his head and motions to another man, who rises slowly, as if this is an imposition. How long? "*Casi veinte años.*" Almost twenty years.

The guards look at each other and shrug. One of them asks Daddy for a smoke. Our driver, waiting at the curb, opens the car door and whistles to get the guards' attention. "*Oye, hombre,*"—Listen, man—"what's the problem here?"

"*Nada, nada.*" It's nothing. He lets us go after extracting two cigarettes from the wrinkled pack that Daddy offers. We swing out into the roadway. Daddy holds a match to another cigarette and inhales deeply. Mama reaches out and touches my shoulder like she can't believe I'm here, can't believe that I didn't disappear like Berta. She's saying "my precious baby" over and over again, and I kiss her damp cheek with its etching of worry lines. I sink my face against her hair, wishing I could smooth her anxiety away.

I ask how things are in the capital. Mama lowers her voice as if we're still in the Trujillo years and says it's too soon to tell but there are rumors of a *golpe*, a coup. I guess that explains the armed guards.

"It's nothing for you to worry about, darling." She pats my hand. "Let's not talk about that."

"We'll just sit tight, as always," Daddy says. He lights another cigarette and takes a couple of deep drags. I fall asleep in the car for a while with my head against Mama's shoulder. She shakes me awake to see the lights of Miches spread out below like a tattered shawl spun of gold, pocked by black holes. As we pass the town square by the church, I look for familiar faces, but the streets are empty. It's suppertime. Charcoal fires hint of roasting meat and boiling stews. We dodge a sleeping dog and a flock of pigeons and then we're home. Once inside, Casalata looks tiny. I'm a giant in my bedroom, Alice in Wonderland falling down some strange hole that's all shrunken, foreign and familiar at the same time. Berta's bed is being used for storage now. A row of cardboard boxes perch on her mattress, carefully labeled—*finca* business, accounting records. I'm suddenly near tears. I should be used to having this room all to myself by now, but I still want to keep Berta's space ready for her, bed made and mosquito netting ready to protect her from stinging insects.

The sky turns black outside and begins to hum with small night sounds as I unpack. Daddy says "Come sit with us on the porch," so I do. My stomach tightens up in the old way at the sight of the rum bottle. Just like that, it's like I never left, and now Casalata expands and I get smaller and smaller. I will myself to breathe in, out, in like Beth taught me when I said I didn't know what it meant to relax.

The next morning my friends descend on me like a flock of bright parrots, pecking me with sweet kisses until my head spins with joy. They shower me with the latest gossip, and they all want to know if I have an American boyfriend. I say "sort of" and tell them all about Steve and how in America we can go on dates alone with boys. "Ay," Matilde sighs. "If only we could."

We make plans for a fiesta at Maria Antonia's bar that night. A new boy joins us, a university student visiting from Santo Domingo. I remember Luís vaguely; he was a few years older than me and used to try to court Berta but Daddy of course wouldn't allow it. As he walks over to the table, I suddenly forget about Steve. Luís is now quite grown up, his eyes dark and intense. He stares at me.

"*Mírate*," he says. Look at you. Then he sits, still staring. He's almost as tall as Daddy, over six feet, I guess. My stomach grips as if I'm on a roller coaster about to plunge into a free-fall. I give a quick look, almost afraid to be hit by the electric tingling that happens when our eyes meet. I never felt like this with Steve, even if he was the first and only boy I've kissed. It's as if my body just woke up for the first time.

When the jukebox plays a romantic bolero, Luís holds out his hand for a dance. His arm glides around my waist and sparks zing through the empty space between us. My eyes are glued to a button on his white *guayabera* shirt. I glance upward and watch a bead of sweat course down his neck. I have a sudden desire to lick it, but instead move away as if the thought alone is dangerous. His arm tightens around my back and when the music stops we separate quickly, both suddenly awkward. His eyes, soft and hot at the same time, look straight into mine, through all defenses, and I know he feels the same current I do.

Mama and Daddy leave the party at about ten; they've been at another table with the Candelarios. I can stay for another hour. After the rest of the parents leave, our group rearranges itself so sweethearts can sit close together without undue notice from those on chaperone duty. On the next dance I rest my head on Luís's shoulder. The pulse in his neck beats fast and his jawline presses against my hair. He keeps his hips slightly away from actual contact but I can't help but feel his erection every now and then. Most Dominican boys I dance with get them during slow dances. In Miches, erections are like goose bumps, or pimples. They come and go—just the natural consequence of bodies in close proximity. Luís pulls me closer, and I tremble. I don't want to be anywhere else, but someone looks at a watch and announces it's almost midnight. Like a school of startled fish, our group rises as one and flows out to the street. With Luís walking beside me, I float a few inches off the ground. We don't hold hands—no one does. That's against the rules. Whoever made up the rules, however, didn't include dancing as a forbidden act. Which doesn't make any sense, but that's Miches. The escorting party stops a few yards away from Casalata.

"I'll take you the rest of the way," Luís whispers, and we step away from the tinkle of laughter and into the shadows. A quarter moon and a universe of stars prick the darkness. Luís puts his arm around my shoulder and I'm suddenly afraid of how late it is, and maybe Daddy is still up, mad at me for being late. I worry he'll see Luís—just him, alone, not the rest of the gang—so I back away and step into the safety of the yard.

"*Gracias*," I whisper. "I can't stay." Luís reaches over the gate and holds my hand for a moment; his palms are electric, hot.

"*Buenas noches; que duermas bien*," he says, his voice thick like cream. Good night; sleep well. He says he'll be back in town next Sunday for a beach picnic at Playa Arriba, and will I come? I say yes and run to the house, relieved to hear Daddy's snores. The next week one of my friends hands me a small envelope from Luís. "Must be a love letter." She makes kissy noises and I grab the note and stuff it in a pocket.

"You're being silly," I say, but my face is red. Later I race out to our pier and open the envelope. He misses me; he can't wait to see me. I read it over at least a dozen times, then rip it up and toss the pieces in the bay. Like confetti, the white bits swirl in the ripples, and a small fish leaps into the shreds, thinking it's a meal. Suddenly the rickety dock sways, and Mama and Daddy arrive with drinks to watch the sunset. I draw their attention to a spectacular thunderhead lit purple and gold by the setting sun, but I don't have to worry; by now the bay has swallowed the evidence of my forbidden letter.

On the morning of the picnic, a dozen or so people are scattered along the shore, playing games or tending a bonfire. Luís has climbed one of the coconut palms that rim the beach and is knocking off green drinking coconuts with a machete. He grips the swaying trunk with his knees, and I feel weak in the knees myself. He slips the machete into its sheath before skidding backward and jumping onto the soft sand. "I was waiting for you." His chest is smooth and firm and dark hairs disappear into the waistband of his shorts. I swallow hard and pick up a coconut and carry it over to the fire pit where a chicken *sancocho* bubbles away.

The sun beats down and most of the picnickers sit under the shade of *almendra* trees or splash in the bay, waiting for the food to be ready. I join the other bathers, then break away to swim alone out into the cooler deep water. Luís races up behind me. His legs surround mine, holding me tight as we bob in the hard, shimmering light. When I think I might drown from this new sensation, we break apart and stroke ashore, mingling again with the rest of the group. I pretend we'd just been having a little race to see who could swim the farthest without getting tired. On the beach, Luís and I can't touch each other, but something almost unbearable is vibrating between us even so. One of my friends asks me if I'm cold from the water, since I'm shivering. I say yes. We all dig into bowls of stew and I manage to stop shaking. At the end of the day, we all gather up our belongings for the walk home. Mama and Daddy are returning from our pier when I come inside the house.

"How was the beach?"

"Good," I answer, and tell them all about the delicious *sancocho*, and that I've brought them a chunk of *dulce*. I'm red with sunburn and a strange other heat that simmers just below the surface. Later, when they are on the porch with their drinks, I hear my name in their conversation. They don't know I can hear them from the next room.

"She's fine." Mama's voice is sharp, impatient.

"Well, I don't know," Daddy says, sounding serious. "She's never seemed interested in boys, and here she's been gone to Florida for a whole year. She's growing up, but I'm beginning to wonder if maybe, she's, you know . . ."

"Oh, dear." Mama sounds weary, like they've had this talk before. *What*, I wonder, *I'm what?* And then it hits me. Daddy thinks I like girls—because I don't talk about boys, he thinks

I'm like Mary at school with the chopped off hair and shirts that look like they are from the boys' section at Sears. I retreat to my room. I give up. No matter what I do, or don't do, there's going to be something wrong with me. That night I dream that I sneak my bicycle out and meet Luís under the pier. I have the sensation that my lips are swelling as I nip the end of his tongue with my teeth. And then the fear pours in like a sudden storm and Daddy's voice bounces inside my head until all I can hear is the shouts of "Whore, whore—you made your bed and you goddamn well have to lie in it." Just like Daddy yelled at Berta. I can't stop the voice so I pull away from Luís and ride home, pedaling faster and faster, and then I'm tangled up between sleep and not-sleep and wake with a jolt. I'm startled; none of this happened and I'm alone in my bed, sweating and twisted up in the sheets. I lie like a mummy in my cocoon until my heartbeat slows and all that's left is a dull ache.

Luís leaves town to meet with his professors in case the university in the capital gets shut down again. We promise to see each other next year. He gives me a small black-and-white picture of himself looking straight at the camera. I wrap it in a fold of paper and hide it away in my suitcase. As the weeks pass, my fear of Daddy stays at a simmer most of the time, not the feverish boil it used to be, the kind where I bubbled away until I was reduced to nothing and I turned black and smoky inside. It was then I'd get sick with the *gripe*, or the toothaches would start, and I would be allowed to stay in bed until I rested enough to fill up the pot again with another batch of anxiety. Now on bad nights I'm still a prisoner here, but I can escape into thoughts as Daddy winds up about the damn this or the damn that. I pretend to pay attention, but inside my head I pop open the suitcase latch, and slip into my new memories like a coat of armor. When I do that, Casalata and Mama and Daddy shrink again in size.

A letter from Beth arrives in August. A hint of Jean Naté cologne still clings to the envelope after a month in transit. She always sprays letters to Charlie, "So he'll think of me." I splash happily through two pages of news and gossip—lots about Charlie, but not a word about Steve. I figure that means he's dating someone else. I feel a twinge of sadness when I read that Beth's parents have decided not to send her back to Howey for her junior year. The money they save will go toward her college fund. She'll miss me; she'll never forget me; we're forever friends. I must come to her home for visits, okay?

Before I leave Miches, I remember the painting nailed to the back of the cabinet in Daddy's workshop, the portrait of Berta and me painted in Spain when she was six and I was two. I ask Daddy if I can take it with me to Florida. "Sure," he says, "help yourself." He sounds surprised, as if he's forgotten it is still there. He doesn't spend much time in the workshop anymore. He long ago stopped making jewelry, and has constructed everything that needed building. Now he uses the workbench just to fix things that break or wear out. The garage still smells like copra, but added to that is the odor of rust and decay, of aging and giving up. The cabinet door opens with a squeak. The portrait has a glaze of cobwebs and dust. Daddy pulls out the rusted tacks from the corners and rolls it up into a cylinder. "You know, it's not a good painting," he says as he hands it to over me.

"That's okay," I say. I brush away some dirt and Berta's blue eyes stare at me, her short blonde hair pulled back with two bows. I feel tears welling up as I pack it carefully in my suitcase. I just hope the corroded tack holes, which remind me of the punctures in paintings of Jesus on the cross, can be concealed when I clean it up and stretch it into a new frame. Maybe Mama and Daddy don't want to remember, but I want to know there was a time before innocence collapsed, when we wore shiny bows in our hair and an artist painted us.

My departure from the island is delayed by another hurricane. The bay once again is a frenzy of whitecaps, and the wind sandpapers my skin. In the last big storm, so soon after Berta disappeared, I wanted to be swallowed up by the waves, but now I fantasize that Luís is here in the nick of time, pulling me away from danger and into his protective arms. I think storms and love must be the same; they disturb everything, changing landscapes overnight, opening and breaking hearts. I don't know yet about the other storm that waits in the offing to turn our lives inside out and rearrange them in entirely different pieces.

Chapter Twenty-Two

※

Bombshells

On a cool October morning I'm with the rest of the junior class taking PSAT tests when the door opens and a teacher tiptoes up to the woman administering the tests. We look up in unison, glad for any interruption of the task in front of us. The teacher nods and walks to my desk. I'm to go to Mr. McFarland's office—yes, now—she'll arrange for me to retake the test later. I have visitors. I'm puzzled—who would be visiting me? When I walk into his office I see two strangers, an older couple, perched on the couch as if at attention. A small boy about three years old huddles between them.

Mr. McFarland takes my arm and gestures towards the trio. "These are your sister's in-laws—and this—well." He pauses. "This is your nephew."

I try to absorb the words but his voice is suddenly coming from someplace far away and I can only make out faint sounds as mouths open and close. Mr. McFarland's grip gets tighter. I can't move. Then an anguished yelp comes out from some place deep in my gut and I stumble before Mr. McFarland edges me into a chair. I watch as if from a vast distance as the tow-haired child picks up a tissue from a box on the table and toddles over to me. "Don't cwy." Stubby little fingers thrust the white square into my shaking hand. In his clear blue eyes I see Berta in there, peering at me, alive and curious.

The two older people sit like rocks, as if realizing they've made a mistake coming here. I try to stop the tears and reach out and touch the downy hair. "I'm sorry I'm crying. I just—I am glad to meet you, really." I move my chin in the direction of the statues on the couch to include them as well. I take a ragged breath. "What's your name?" and he tells me. Mitch. As if I don't know his name, as if I haven't imagined holding him from the time his father found him in the crib, alone, with his mother gone, gone. As if I haven't looked for him in every infant, then every small child I've come across anywhere in Florida, even here. As if I haven't screamed silently, *Are you him? Are you?* and their mothers haven't caught me watching and turned away, uncomfortable at this girl just staring into their precious child's eyes. They can't know I'm looking, always looking, for these very same blue eyes.

I have no idea how Scott's parents knew to find me here or why they came. The woman clears her throat. She explains that a long time ago Berta had given them the Breedens' address. From them, they'd learned I was attending this school. "I—we —just thought you'd like to, you know, see Mitch. He lives with us now, ever since—well, he's just an angel, such a good boy."

Mitch lets me pull him into my lap. His back presses into me with little boy smells of soap and potato chips. He turns his face up to mine. "Who you?"

"Your aunt." I run my fingers all over his face, memorizing his cheeks and ears like a blind person. Please don't ask me what an aunt is, I pray. He doesn't. He lets me explore him like an unknown world and when he's had enough he squirms down off the chair. I let him go and his attention focuses again on his grandmother. "I'm hungry."

They leave after scribbling their address on a piece of paper and saying they'll write me if I'd like that. I don't know, I say. I don't know. I manage to hold my tears back as I hug Mitch and give him a big smile good-bye so he can see his aunt is happy. They wave and the car disappears beyond the pines with their shrouds of Spanish moss. Mr. McFarland tells me to stay put and a cup of tea appears. He makes some telephone calls, to the office, to let them know I won't be in class for the rest of the day. I sit in the chair, staring into a territory I can't place where Berta appears and disappears like the Cheshire cat, only it's her blue eyes, not a grin, that fade in and out. The sky darkens and a damp rain whispers outside.

The next day is Saturday, so I can hide my swollen face in the room all day. I lose my voice for three days. I don't write Scott's parents. Instead I throw away their address. When a letter from Mama arrives, I think I'll write her about Mitch, but then I start shaking and somehow I know it's a secret I have to keep. Instead I respond to her news—they got hit hard by Hurricane Flora, which killed over seven thousand in the Caribbean. Cocoloco didn't lose too many trees, but rivers were impassable for weeks. She writes that the musical chairs are starting again in the capital; she doesn't have to tell me what

that means. I write only that I'm glad they're safe. I can't think
of anything else to say.

On a chilly Friday in November someone screams that
President Kennedy has been shot. All classes stop. Students sit
numb in front of television sets in the recreation room and
watch as the television replays the motorcade scene, in black
and white, over and over again. It doesn't seem real. I catch Mrs.
Hitchens sobbing in her room, and my Spanish teacher keeps
blowing her nose. From that week on, there's no longer any
certainty about anything, anywhere. I feel like I'm in a bad
dream where I'm struggling to stay afloat on a raft in a stormy
ocean. There is no tether to shore, no strong hands to pull me in
to safety. Even Mr. McFarland breaks down in the special Sunday
service, his jaw quivering and his voice fading in and out.

In the midst of this strange time, Mr. Geddes' art studio is a
safe harbor, so now, every day after class, the art students come
together. Here I find a community of other refugees; we aren't the
captains of basketball teams or leaders of the cheerleading squad.
We're loners, the shy ones, or we get good grades. But in this
sanctuary, the heady smell of oils and turpentine wipe away some
of our anxieties or fears. Here I can stop thinking about
Kennedy's assassination, about Berta, about the small blonde boy,
and about the continuing turmoil at home after Trujillo's killing.

I make friends with Pam, another artist. We listen over and
over to her Beatles records while I draw portraits of the floppy-
haired singers. Pam says she's in love with John Lennon, so I do
a rendering of John with colored chalks and she buys it and
posts it on her bedroom wall. It's my first art sale.

In Mr. Geddes' room I lose myself for hours, painting
furiously and filling canvas after canvas. Not knowing why, I
start painting women in provocative poses with exposed

cleavage and eyes daring, staring out from the canvas. They have long hair and large breasts—they are everything I'm not. They emerge in harsh scrapes of the palette knife and broad brush strokes and leap into being: hungry, eyes looking straight on. Week after week I pile on the colors on my palette: burnt umber, yellow ochre, ultramarine, alizarin crimson, Payne's gray. My painting technique is awkward at first, and the proportions are wrong, but something happens and the canvases come alive. When the Art Club has its annual sale I sell more paintings than anyone else. The buyers are all men.

At the end of the sale, Mr. Geddes hands me a check with a sparkle in his eye. It might as well be a million dollars. I know one thing, finally, about myself. I'm an artist. I begin painting self-portraits, and they don't look like my other works at all. In these I'm only halfway visible, behind a wall or with my face turned partly away, just like I used to draw in Miches. Mr. Geddes says I'm good enough to earn a scholarship if I want to study in France after high school. He says to keep painting and that we'll explore this further in my senior year. I write my parents with this good news. They respond that I shouldn't get any foolish ideas. Things are unstable, they can't afford anything like that anyway, and besides, they've shown some of the landscapes I painted back in Miches to friends who know about art, and really, I'm not that talented. *Make sure you take typing and shorthand*, the letter ends.

I don't see Luís the summer after my junior year; he doesn't come to Miches and no one knows why. Back at school I start to get letters from him with a Puerto Rico return address. He writes, *Mi querida*. My dear one. He explains he had to stay with relatives all summer to escape being a target by the Dominican government.

"Don't mention anything that I'm going to tell you—it could be dangerous for both of us." My throat closes up. He writes that communist revolutionaries are planning an overthrow of the Dominican government, and university students are being arrested for inciting disturbances. He says one student was shot and killed by the *policía militar*. He's staying away from the country for now. He ends by saying how glad he is that I'm safe in Florida, that he misses me more each day.

A letter from Mama arrives a month later. The envelope has obviously been opened and is resealed with dirty Scotch tape. I remember Luís writing that all letters to the US are being opened by the Dominican government now. It's just one page. The cleanup from the storms is complete, and workers have replaced some damaged trees with new sprouts. The outboard engine is acting up and Daddy's trying to fix it, but so far no luck. She hopes my studies are going well and wants me to write about my new roommate. *Take care of yourself, darling*, the letter ends.

Dear Mama and Daddy, I got your letter yesterday. I'm Vice President of the Art Colony this year and still on the National Honor Society. You asked about my new roommate. Denise is from Melbourne—that's Florida, not Australia, ha ha. I met her parents last month. Her dad is an engineer at the Kennedy Space Center. He's working on this huge building called the VAB where they'll assemble the new rockets. She says it will be so tall it will have its own weather system—inside. Can you imagine that? She also said Cape Kennedy is crawling with alligators and that her dad had to chase one away from under his car last summer. Anyway, Denise and I are getting along fine. She's a little moody, but I'm sure as she makes more friends, she'll perk up. Well, the supper bell just rang, and here's Denise, so I'll finish this later.

DENISE HENRY IS ALWAYS HERE. She's short, with wispy black hair and pale green eyes. I don't tell Mama and Daddy about how she clings to me as if I'm the only lifeboat in her stormy sea. Last night she cried and said it's hard for her to make friends and that it's all because she's adopted. She's told me this twice now, how she doesn't fit in, even in her own family. I'm sorry she's miserable, but I'm starting to feel suffocated. It's hard to escape Denise: she waits for me before meals and sits next to me in the classes we share. I begin to plot ways to avoid her without her catching on. One night I have a nightmare about something that happened in Miches a long time ago when I was playing in the ocean with a friend. She got scared when a big wave surprised us and grabbed onto my neck because she couldn't swim. I slipped off a rock and she wouldn't let go and I almost drowned. In the dream it's Denise that's choking me underwater and I sputter awake, heart jumping.

In December I put my name on the list of students needing housing over the Christmas break. Denise discovers I won't be going to Miches for Christmas and claps her hands in excitement. "Oh, goody—you can come home with me—it will be wonderful!"

With no good reason not to accept her offer, I console myself by thinking it won't be that bad. I'll be with her entire family; they'll be like a buffer zone or something. Mr. Henry picks us up in a station wagon, and three hours later the Atlantic is ahead, gunmetal gray under the watery sun. Mr. Henry points north to Cape Kennedy and says that is the center of the world, right there. "This is where we'll shoot men off to the moon."

In Miches, when I was younger, we knew of the missiles being hurled into space from somewhere in Florida. Because the Dominican Republic was on their trajectory, sometimes we'd see spectacular streaks flying across the night sky, too huge to be falling stars. Once Daddy and I saw a large flash explode over the horizon. As I look at the Cape, now so close, I think of President Kennedy's speech about landing a man on the moon before the decade is out. I never believed it before, but it's looking like it could happen. I remember Daddy's comment that soon there won't be enough room on earth so we'll need to live on the moon. He said that when the wife of one of his workers died giving birth to her eighth child.

At Cocoa Beach we turn south by bars and restaurants with space themes—The Orbit Lounge, Rocket Red's, Comet Café. The Henrys live in a large subdivision filled with identical houses a few blocks in from the beach. They insist I call them by their first names, Ron and June. Denise says her dad has top-secret clearance at work. June is magazine-pretty and blonde. Clairol, Denise says, rolling her eyes. I take it she doesn't approve. Denise's younger sister Patricia has a stream of friends flowing in and out of her room.

Denise, I note with a sinking feeling, doesn't seem to have any friends, except her boyfriend Tom—and me. Tom's stocky and wears a military-style haircut. I can't see what Denise finds attractive in him, except that he pays attention to her. He is a computer technician, also working at the Cape. "You just wait," she says. "We'll be engaged by next year; you'll see."

Ron and June don't seem to notice Denise's mood swings, or maybe they are just used to it. I'm just glad when we're back in school and I can find ways to escape her. In March Luís writes that the noose is tightening in Santo Domingo. I'm not sure what he means by that, but it sounds ominous. He finishes by warning that this may be the last letter he can send me, but summer is only three months away so we'll be seeing each other soon in Miches.

By April all the Florida papers are full of Dominican news because a new military junta has taken power. The American news reports change daily, and with rioting mobs and bombs, the death toll is rising daily. Dominican warplanes strafe the governmental palace with machine-gun fire and electricity is cut off in Santo Domingo. I pretend none of this has anything to do with Miches. My friends will stay in the village until this storm passes. I tell myself I'm sure Luís is safe. Mama and Daddy know better than to go to the capital city, so they'll be fine, too. But I can't shake the queasiness; sleep brings nightmares, and I wake up with a heavy weight below my rib cage that never seems to go away.

The dread gets worse after I hear President Johnson has ordered the evacuation of all Americans from the Dominican Republic. I'm glued to the television news every night. Hundreds of Marines land on the island and thousands more military troops will be deployed in the days ahead. The news shows masses of young men in fatigues and helmets exiting airplanes and ships. It's like watching a war movie, but with the familiar backdrop of the Dominican coastline. Palm trees wave in the breeze as always. Small boys in tattered pants surround the soldiers, as they do any foreigners, hands extended for *cheles* —pennies—or candy. In the weeks that follow, I remain in a daze. In class I see the teacher's lips move but only a few words sink into my brain. In the cafeteria line, someone prods me to move along. I didn't know I'd stopped and was just staring at the Jell-O in the metal tray. It's easiest not to believe what I'm seeing and reading. I tell myself that by June all this will blow over like a hurricane, and as usual, I'll go home—this time for good.

The call from Norma Breeden comes on a Tuesday, just after a history class. I'm summoned to the office, where I pick up the telephone. Norma's voice is almost hysterical. She's calling from Miami. She wants to know whether my parents have been safely evacuated. She doesn't stop for breath or my answer. "We got out just in the nick of time. It's awful, really awful. We had to leave everything." She starts crying, and then Ed gets on the phone. I tell him I've heard nothing, not even a letter, since late March.

The telephone is silent for a minute, and I say "Hello, *hello?*" thinking we may have gotten cut off and I don't know how to reach them again. My own voice rises into a breathless whine. "Are you there?" I'm lightheaded, afraid I'll drop the phone.

"We're right here." Ed's tone is calm; it reminds me of Walter Cronkite's voice when he's on the TV news, croaky but sincere. "I'm sure you'll hear something soon. Call us when you know where they landed." My fingers tremble as I write down their telephone number. In the dark of the insulated dorm room, after lights out, I claw my skin until it bleeds, as if hurting myself will stop the panic. It doesn't.

By the end of the week President Johnson has ordered thousands more Marines to the Dominican Republic. A refugee zone is set up in Santo Domingo for all foreign embassies. From here ships and planes will take the foreigners away to safety. That's how the Breedens got out. The school puts me in touch with the Dominican embassy in Miami. I give them my parents' names, and one official promises to inquire if my parents have made it to the safe zone. He says he'll back in touch with me soon. Mr. McFarland also helps me make calls to different American officials, but no one can tell me anything more, or what to do.

On the island, battles continue into May. I hear no word from anyone about my parents. Telephone communication to the Dominican Republic is now cut off entirely. Except for a few students, expats like me, no one else seems aware of the situation. I meet with the dean, and he asks me if there is anyone I can stay with in the States if things, as he puts it, "get sticky" for my return home. I say no. By now over a thousand are dead in the country. The war is spreading far beyond the city, and guerrilla fighters are now organizing in the mountains to the north. That's getting very close to Miches.

Chapter Twenty-Three

Graduation

Graduation looms and I've not heard back from any US officials. Norma and Ed Breeden stop calling. No longer able to pretend everything will be all right soon, I sink into a state of shock and lethargy. Outside everything is brittle and bright, but inside it feels like I'm looking through a shroud, the kind that Dominicans wear when they are in mourning, veils that keep their grief inside. I try to cover up the worry that wells up at night because if I let the worry have its way it turns into panic and I begin to sweat and it's all I can do to keep myself from exploding. When I'm wet and shaking from panic, sometimes I think I want to be dead because it hurts so much to be alive. So I hold tight and try to pull all the bad thoughts back inside so I can breathe again. So I can pretend I'm okay.

School closes down for the summer in two weeks, and no one knows what to do with me. I sure don't. Denise has the solution to my problem: her family will be delighted to have me come live with them for a while. More numb than grateful, I accept. It doesn't seem that I have any control over my fate, and besides, Denise has it all figured out. We'll get summer jobs together. I swallow my dread and try to sound thankful. That won't be necessary; I tell her. I'll hear from my family soon. Before graduation. Just in the nick of time. You'll see.

My Aunt Betty flies in from New York to come to my graduation. She's Mama's older sister, and I've only seen her once in fifteen years, the time we took a trip to the States when I was twelve. I step up to the podium in the bright sunshine and accept my diploma. I'm graduating *magna cum laude*, fourth in my senior class. The headmaster beams at me as he hands me the scroll. "Your family will be very proud," he says. I try to smile, but I can barely see him through a cloud of tears. I fumble my way to Aunt Betty; she hugs me tight. Daddy and Mama would be proud, indeed. So would Berta, wouldn't she?

Aunt Betty's mouth is moving, but I can't hear her in the chaos of flying caps and balloons and all-around jubilation. Our steps crunch on the gravel outside the school, where a procession of taxis and cars lie in wait, ready to take their charges to airports, buses, home. Shouts of relief and joy punctuate the still air as students charge out of the buildings for the last time, hugging classmates and promising again and again to write. A boarding school is like an island—we all waded ashore from somewhere and were stranded together for years. Now it is time to leave. I walk my aunt to the waiting taxi. Her hair, like Mama's, is silver-white. It's nicely styled, unlike

Mama's no-nonsense cut, which is always kept in check by an uneven pattern of bobby pins. Aunt Betty's voice is low and sweet as she says she'll keep in touch. My stomach hurts and I feel like I'm in quicksand. I want to scream out my fears of being left alone, of not knowing what to do except get in the Henrys' waiting station wagon with Denise. I want Aunt Betty to say, *Wait, I've changed my mind—come up with me to Port Washington. Sue will be so glad to see you.* Sue is my cousin, another almost-stranger I exchange Christmas cards with every year. But I know Aunt Betty can't take me in no matter how much I wish it.

The sun glints white-hot off the taxi and I pull myself together, blink away tears, and pretend a smile. Aunt Betty whispers "Be brave" and pats my back. "You'll be fine. The Henrys seem like very nice people and it's awfully good you'll be with your roommate. You're quite lucky."

I nod, my eyes stinging. For a minute or so, I stay paralyzed in one spot. The taxi leaves. Other cars slide around me, jockeying for position. Trunks snap open, car doors slam. Squeals and greetings and good-byes mix with the smell of exhaust and swirls of dust. Planting one foot carefully in front of the other, I slowly traverse what seems now to be a very long distance back to the front door of the school.

"There you are!" Denise bounds up to me. "Dad's loading my stuff in the car," she announces. "How soon will you be finished packing?"

I steady myself and say I'll see her downstairs in a half hour. I step into the cool, old-wood smell inside. I climb the stairs slowly, gripping the banister, and sink onto my bed. The room is empty, except for my suitcase, which is mostly packed. The air is stale with the scent of faded varnish and the peculiar tint of silence. I check all the drawers and find a small box with some letters, a few drawings, and a folded piece of cardboard that protects my treasure, the picture of Luís. I whisper his name, my voice choking, then bury my head in the pillow. I'll see you soon, I promise the small picture. It won't be long. This storm in Santo Domingo will blow over, like the others always do. I close my eyes and imagine Mama and Daddy, sitting on the porch right now. I just know they are okay; they wouldn't leave Miches.

Chaplain McFarland has promised to check for any mail from home. "My father's stubborn," I tell him. "They'll get in touch with me soon, and I'll go home."

"What will you do then?" he asks.

"I don't know," I answer, surprised by the question. "Whatever they decide, I guess." He looks at me oddly. "You just graduated from high school. You must have some idea of what you'd like to do next."

What I'd like to do? That thought never occurs to me, it just bounces off my mind like a stone thrown at a rock wall. I never decide anything; I'm not allowed to. I can type and take shorthand. Maybe I'll be a typist at an American company or the Embassy, or something like that in the capital. Before now, I thought maybe the Breedens would rent me their guest room in Santo Domingo, but they're gone, so that won't work. I will myself to get up. It is time to make believe all is well.

In Melbourne, I take babysitting jobs and wait for word from home. Weekly, I call the school and the various government officials. I call the Breedens. "Oh, honey," Norma says with a moan, "No matter what happens, we're not going back. Ed thinks it will be years before American businesses will be welcome again." I stop calling her; she's not helping my state of mind. I have no money and the Henrys have been supporting me for two months. I give them my babysitting cash and June puts it back in my hand, shaking her head, no, no. Don't worry about it.

Still I wait. Denise and I drive up to Brevard Junior College so she can register. When we get back to Melbourne, June runs out. "The school called, they have news of your parents. They're okay." Of course they are. Relief streaks through me like lightning, filling my hollow places. I dial the Howey number. My mind is racing; I'm already half-packed in my mind. My head is buzzing with excitement. Finally, Mr. McFarland is on the line with a ham radio message my parents have sent. The message is very short, saying they're fine and that once they establish my whereabouts they'll contact me more directly. I feel light, like I'm almost floating, when I finally get an actual letter from Mama. She's relieved I'm with the Henrys. *Please let them know how much we appreciate their taking you in*, she writes, and then: *We miss you terribly, but I'm afraid it's not safe for you to come home now.* I take a deep breath. Okay, I can wait a few months. This is not a problem.

The letter continues: *I'm sorry to say this, but you're just going to have to stay in the States and make your own way.* Panic grips my throat as I try to swallow the words, to make them go down, but they rise like bile, green, ugly. I reread the sentence as if the words will change on the page, poof, like magic. Instead I can see Mama brushing the sweat off her face and lighting a cigarette to steady herself as she tips me over the edge of the cliff. As if I know how to fly, as if anyone ever taught me to flap my wings and fly to the next branch, to a new life. The paper swims in front of my eyes. I brush aside dread and finish reading.

I wish we could help with money, but we can't, not now anyway. Maybe things will be stable enough for you to come home for a visit at Christmas. We'll just have to see.

Denise enters the room. "So, when are you leaving?" It's almost an accusation. I just stare at her, then back at the piece of paper. My world has collapsed again to this room, to Denise. She will be happy with the news, glad to have me once again all to herself. I crawl under the covers in the hot, sticky afternoon. I can't cry. I escape into sleep and wake up to June's hands checking to see if I have a fever. I give her the note.

She shakes her head as she reads, then tells me I can stay until I get my feet on the ground. "We like having you, and you're such good company for Denise."

The sky crackles with lightning and thunder booms as a huge rainstorm turns the sky black. I slip out of the house and let the wind lacerate me with flying sand. I stumble along the path to the beach and lie face-up to the sky, watching clouds race and boil. A jolt of lightning, too close, sends me crawling back to the house and back into bed, where I curl up into a ball and throw up.

I enroll at Brevard Junior College and get a night job in the credit department at Sears. I begin paying rent to the Henrys and can take care of my school expenses. Letters begin to flow back and forth from Miches. Most of the US troops have left, and the Embassy has reopened. It looks like I'll be able to come home for a two-week visit over Christmas. Slowly, slowly, the knots in my stomach start to loosen up. I'm going home. To celebrate, I put a matched set of Sears luggage on layaway. The color is lipstick red. Daddy will think it's too loud, but I don't care. I've already been kicked out of home, in a way, so what is he going to do?

Chapter Twenty-Four

✳

Nightmare on King Street

Denise and Tom are waiting to pick me up at the Orlando airport after my Christmas visit to Miches, my first time home in a year and a half. As I'd suspected, Daddy had waved away the American military helicopters that landed at Cocoloco to rescue them. Mama says he told them to go to hell. I close my eyes and hear Daddy again: "Dammit, we made it through the Trujillo years, and what is an old American farmer anyway to all these crazy people who want to take over the country? Let them fight. I make do; I always do." Even now, back in Florida, I want to scream at Mama, whose hair is now entirely white, *What about you? What do you think or feel? Look at you—you're half-dead.* But of course I'd never say that to her. When I'm in Miches it's like an old lock gets clamped over my mouth, making it impossible to speak.

"Guess what?" Denise yells, jumping up and down and thrusting her left hand in my face. I will myself to come back to the present. I'm in Florida again, back to life with the Henrys, with Denise. I pull my baggage off the carousel.

"C'mon, guess!" She doesn't wait for an answer and does a little pirouette that almost knocks my suitcase to the ground. "We got married on Christmas and moved to Rockridge yesterday! We just got an apartment—and the best news of all is, you're moving in with us!" She shoves her finger at me so I can see the wedding band. Tom grins too and displays a matching flash of gold.

"What?" I stutter. I can't believe my ears, my eyes. I swallow the lump that is stuck in my throat.

Tom picks up my suitcases. "As a matter of fact"—he pauses like an actor who's been rehearsing his speech for dramatic effect—"that's where we're headed tonight. We already moved most of our things, plus your stuff too. You'll get to spend your first night back in our new apartment. It's not far from the college."

They both rattle on and I move my feet slowly, like a zombie. I want to run back onto the tarmac and get on a plane, as if it's that easy; as if I have somewhere else to go. Denise has obviously been planning this for months, but has saved the surprise for now. I expect she's calculated that what I pay her parents will just as easily take care of a portion of the rent for their new apartment. Now she has everything she's wanted— her own place, Tom, and me.

"HONEY, WE'RE HOME!" Tom cackles and lifts Denise up in the air. She laughs in the cold light of the fluorescent sign that indicates we have arrived at the King Street Apartments—

Affordable Living on the Space Coast. No Leases Required. Pets OK.
It's 1:30 a.m. The two-bedroom apartment is on the second
floor in a complex of barrack-like structures painted gray with
black trim. Cigarette butts litter the stairwell, where a swarm of
insects flutter around a light. The screen door has holes in it big
enough to let a bat fly through. Denise says the landlord will
replace it this week. My room has barely enough space for a
twin bed and the old dresser I used at the Henrys. A small
window looks across a narrow alley to an identical building
beyond. I try to open it but the mildewed metal frame is stuck.
It's larger than my room in Miches but feels like a jail cell.

As the days pass, Denise takes control of everything. Tom
goes to work and then sprawls on the couch watching television
until dinnertime. Denise and I go to school together, get
groceries together, do our laundry together. The couple doesn't
act like any newlyweds I've read about or seen in the movies.
They don't laugh much and hardly talk to each other. I imagine
they are more like some old couples I see in the Sears coffee
shop at break time, staring into their cups as if there's nothing
left to say.

It wouldn't have been like that with Luís, not that strange
dead space between two people. I write him a farewell letter. I
don't know his address so I mail it to Zuleica, who has promised
to give it to him the next time he's in Miches. *I hope this finds
you well,* I start, then cross it out and just say, *I hope this finds you.*
I tell him I'll never forget him, ever, but that my fate is sealed.
That sounds too dramatic so I cross that line out then scratch it
in again. It's true. I write down my new address and say if this
ever gets to you, write me one last time?

A letter from Luís arrives a month later, the handwriting
filling up all the edges of the paper with a fierce slant forward,

like he's leaning into a storm. It turns out he traveled to Miches the day after I flew back to Florida. He's heartbroken, angry at himself for not getting to Miches sooner. *I had a premonition*, he writes. *And now you're gone.*

And that's the end. Luís is only an idea now, not real. Just a fading photo and some letters. Even if I were living back at home, I couldn't date him without Daddy kicking me out of the house. And if I was a grownup, living in the capital, Daddy would still disown me if I married a Dominican. So there's no point in even thinking about Luís anymore. Instead, I lie in bed at night and think about escaping this prison, but I can't conjure up any kind of a plan. I'm just stuck here. I'm like one of those crabs we used to hunt—a flashlight is blinding me, and I'm waving my pincers but there's no place to hide from the cleaver that will crack me open.

Denise cooks the meals and doesn't want anyone in the kitchen with her, which makes sense because two people don't fit in the L-shaped cubbyhole. After meals I clean up. After dinner I take the bus to my Sears job, and Tom picks me up. I say I'll ride the bus home, but he says, no, that's dangerous, I'll get you. He smokes Marlboro cigarettes and turns up the country music for the fifteen-minute ride back to the apartment.

One morning I wake up early and panic rips through me like a lightning bolt. I don't know why, maybe a bad dream that I can't remember. I feel like the walls are pressing in, suffocating me. I brush my teeth and grab my books. I can smell coffee brewing and it makes me want to throw up. Denise is at the stove. I announce I don't want breakfast and that I'll take the bus to school. I tell her I'm going to have a snack with a girl who is also in my first class of the day, Business 101. I have no such plans. The morning class is one of the few I don't share with Denise, so I invent my new friend. Denise looks at me with a frown and then, without warning, throws the frying pan, eggs and all, right at me. The pan falls short of its mark, clanging to the floor, my shirt dripping runny scrambled eggs.

Tom opens the bathroom door, wiping off shaving cream. "What the hell, Dee?" I just stand there, as if I've done something terrible to cause her outburst.

"It was an accident." Denise's eyes dare me with a flash of green. Tom drops to the floor with his towel to help clean up the mess. He hasn't noticed my soggy clothing. I retreat to my room and shut the door. I rinse out my soiled blouse when Tom finishes shaving, then aim for the door, my mouth dry. Denise is back in the kitchen, cooking up another batch of eggs. She doesn't look up. Tom gives me a puzzled glance and wonders out loud why I'm not eating.

"She's meeting a friend at school." Denise drags out the word *friend* as if it's something dirty.

The bus drops me off near campus and I can't shake the knot in my stomach. Why don't I speak up for myself? Why am I so afraid of Denise? What's the worst she can do—kick me out? I can't think about that right now. I wouldn't know where to go or what to do. But she won't do that anyway. She needs my rent money. Besides, I'm supposed to be grateful for the roof over my head. She's doing me a big favor. My thoughts fuzz up and turn gray and mushy and I stop trying to sort it all out.

Chapter Twenty-Five

※

Resurrection

On a rainy afternoon I'm sprawled across my bed, studying, when I hear the telephone in the living room. It won't be for me, so I ignore it, but it doesn't stop ringing. In the bathroom, the shower shudders to full blast and I realize Denise can't hear the phone either, so I grab a piece of paper to take down a message. An operator is asking for me, and then I hear a woman's voice, faint and far away. It sounds almost like Mama but I'm not sure it is her because we've never spoken on a telephone. My heart skids and I feel the blood rush from my face. I can only imagine something terrible has happened to Daddy; any other news would arrive by letter.

"*Mama?*" I squawk, forcing myself to speak.

"Rita, Rita, is that you?"

"Yes, I'm here. Is it Daddy—what's the matter?"

Her voice fades in and out, and I miss some words. I make out something like Daddy's all right, that's not why she's calling. Then the phone spits static and I shout, "I can't hear you, what did you say?"

The static evaporates and her voice is clear but breathless and shaky. It's about Berta. They got a letter from Berta. She's alive. I'm too numb to make sense of the words. I hear sounds entering my ear, spinning through my head, and Mama's saying, "Can you hear me? Rita?"

I nod as if she can see me.

"Darling, did you hear what I said?" I choke out a strangled *yes*. I don't know what to say; I'm not capable of forming a complete sentence. *Berta?*

"Is she—is she okay?"

Mama's voice falters and I can hear now that she's crying. "She's—she's fine." Mama's voice is still wobbly but maybe it's the phone line. I try to concentrate on the crackling phone line. Mama's saying she's written me a letter so I'll get more details soon. Berta?

"Where is she?" I ask, as if that's important to know instead of why Berta has hidden from us for so many years. All of a sudden I'm hot, boiling angry when I know I should be happy, ecstatic, thrilled.

"Arizona, she's someplace in Arizona." Mama says Berta's letter doesn't give a lot of details. We'll all know more soon, and we should just be thankful. It's a miracle.

"Yes," I say, as my voice quivers. "I just can't believe it."

"I know. It's been quite a shock."

"How's Daddy?"

"He—it's been quite a shock," Mama repeats. The phone line crackles again and Mama says, "Well, I just wanted to call you before you got my letter—" The line is dead and I'm paralyzed, holding the phone, until the automated voice tells me to hang up and I do.

Denise emerges with a towel wrapped around her head. "Was that for me?" I shake my head no, and she says what's wrong, and I say I have wonderful news, then I burst out crying and stumble to my room and fling myself across the bed. I hear her ask Tom what's that all about, and he says he has no idea. The winter light fades and dulls the room into gray inside and out. The rain has slowed to a drizzle and droplets course slowly down the dirty window glass. I watch one drop fill up like a tick gorged on blood, getting fatter until it can't hold itself together and spills into a trail. Thoughts pour through my head. Confusion and anger wrestle with something like relief. I'm supposed to be happy. Why don't I feel happy? I lie there, unable to move, and let the battle rage in my head as my body shivers. *Berta is alive.* I mouth the word, so strange on my tongue. *Alive.* Not dead, not a body plucked out of the surf. Alive. How many years? Does it matter how many when it's a lifetime, when everything has changed forever?

I stare at the raindrops. It is anticlimactic, really, this news. She is already dead, has been dead to Daddy, to Mama, to me for weeks, months, and years, so long that it's all we know. Her being alive after all is stranger than believing she is dead. I close my burning eyes and can see the thin airmail envelope, the kind that weighs almost nothing except for the words inside. It wings out over the Arizona desert and flies east and south, dipping over the Caribbean. I imagine Mama's face when the letter drifts into our village mailbox thousands of miles away, arriving as suddenly as Berta vanished. I see Mama's trembling fingers pressing on that familiar handwriting, so much like Mama's own writing style, each letter rounded and small, yet easy to read. I can imagine her crying out, how maybe she fell to the ground or just stood stock still as if a single movement could make the letter disappear back into thin air.

And Daddy, what about him? After all, he disowned Berta when she was alive, called her those horrible names, erased her from his whole being like she'd never been born. If he didn't want her to exist when she was alive, what is he thinking now? A timid knock on the door interrupts my thoughts. Dinner's ready. I don't answer. Minutes pass, then Denise rattles the doorknob.

"You eating?" She actually sounds concerned. I sit up and the room spins. I squint my swollen eyes, not sure what I'm going to say or do. "It's my sister. She's alive."

"Sister? What sister?"

I forgot—I never told Denise. When we were first roommates, she assumed I was an only child, so I never told her anything different—much easier that way. The room is silent except for the pot of chili bubbling on the stove. Tom sits at the dinette table fiddling with the glass salt and pepper shakers. *Click, click. Click, click.*

Finally I explain what I know and don't know in between spoonfuls of chili. Denise has real tears in her eyes, and I feel the anger seep out of me until I'm just dead tired and can't think or talk anymore. Mama's letter arrives the next week. I was hoping she'd enclose Berta's letter but she doesn't. I expect she couldn't let it go, had to keep it, her only evidence that the long nightmare is really over. Berta is in a small town in Arizona, working at a roadside diner. A family she met at the restaurant has taken her in. From what, I don't know. There is an address; I can write her. She didn't provide a telephone number. Mama says that it might be best if we don't press her. Just be thankful she's reaching out, once again, to her family.

Dear Berta, I start, then stare at the blank page. *How are you?* It's all wrong, I can't find the words. I want to know everything—all the missing parts of her life, so I can fill up the gaping holes in my own. As if getting all the facts is critically important to my survival. A week passes before I manage to write something sanitary, safe, superficial. I don't know this stranger; I don't know that she even wants to hear from me. If she did, she would have written a long time ago.

My words are careful, light. Don't want to scare her away again. My words are timid, whispering over a canyon of missing years. I don't dare look down in the depths below, where emotion cuts its way through cliffs and drowns everything in its path. I want my pen to dig so hard it tears the paper with the real questions: *Why did you leave your baby, your helpless baby? Why did you abandon us too?* But I don't even say, not yet, how much I've missed her. Those words don't even sound true to me. I long ago buried that sentiment in the quicksand inside. I write it would be nice to see her sometime, if she'd like that.

She writes back. She lives with a family who rescued her (she still doesn't say from what), and she's waitressing at a Bob's Big Boy. She encloses a postcard of a roadside diner that sprouts from the desert highway with a towering sculpture of a fat child in red-and-white-checkered apron and pompadour hairstyle. The sculpture is smiling but he looks sinister to me. The landscape surrounding the diner is brown and dusty except for the cactus growing under the statue. Berta sends me her telephone number. When I hear her voice the first time we just weep together until she says I love you and I say I love you, and that's almost too much emotion to handle so we hang up.

Slowly I learn little bits about her life. She's taking classes at night so she can finish high school. But we can only talk about today, not yesterday. It feels like I'm in Daddy's boat on one of our trips to the *finca* when my job was to watch the surface of the water ahead. A slight change in color can be the difference between deep water and a hidden reef that can rip the bottom out of a skiff. Berta's past is like a reef, something to avoid. Sometimes I can't see the danger until I hear her voice turning sharp, then I steer off into safer territory or else she'll hang up. She wants to see me and Mama, but not Daddy, not yet. After a flurry of letters and telephone calls, a reunion is set up in Miami for April. Mama will fly in from Santo Domingo, I'll take the Greyhound. Aunt Betty is coming down from New York too, and the four of us will stay in a hotel near the airport.

THE BUS RUMBLES INTO the Miami station and I hail a cab like a grownup and give the driver the hotel address. Aunt Betty and Mama are already there. Mama has gotten a perm and her white hair is all fluffy. She trembles when we hug. Neither one of us can cry; we're too nervous. By the time Berta's plane lands, we're jittery with adrenaline. Mama wipes her eyes and holds on to her sister's arm so hard I can see the red indents on my aunt's pale wrist. We crowd against the huge glass windows as passengers make their procession across the tarmac and into the terminal. *Is that her? Is that her?*

I don't know if I'm asking it out loud or not but all of a sudden there she is, unmistakably Berta, tall and blonde, walking gingerly. Mama starts moaning and Aunt Betty dispenses Kleenex like a nurse, murmuring, "It's all right, Emily, it's all right."

Mama is shaking so hard I hold on to her and I'm trembling too. Then Berta is right here, close enough to touch. She's wearing a blue shirtwaist dress, her hair curled up at the ends in a wide flip. It's the first time I've seen her in makeup, eyebrows plucked and penciled and black eyeliner making her blue eyes even brighter. She looks pretty, but hard and wary at the same time. Her mouth twitches as if she's trying to speak but can't find words.

We all hug and then Aunt Betty pulls me back so Mama can have her to herself for a minute. She touches Berta's face, learning it again like a blind person using Braille, exploring to be sure everything is still where it needs to be. Berta's eyes are red now. I don't know what to say or do, so we just stare at each other until I look away or she does. Berta doesn't seem real, even though I can smell her hair and her perspiration. I reach out to hold her hand, which is warm and sweaty but I don't care. We spend two strange days full of awkward silences. I'm so hungry to attach again to the sister who left us all behind, to find something I can hold on to. But this is a new person, all prickly and protective like one of the cacti in the Arizona postcards. There isn't enough time to learn where to find the soft places that must still be there behind the armor.

I'm angry but I pretend I'm not because I don't understand the rage that courses through me. Mama stops shaking after one day and slows down on the cigarettes. She smiles, forgiving all. Her pale blue eyes have a sparkle I haven't seen for ages. Berta warms to her and her eyes soften in response, let down their guard for a time. Alone together, Berta and I talk in little fits broken by long silences. I try to grab on to anything that connects me to the dusty years, the mystery years. "Tell me," I plead. "Tell me more. Why not? I'm your sister."

She stiffens. "I can't. I'm sorry I've hurt you; I never meant to."

Long before the end of the reunion it's clear that nothing I can say or do will penetrate beyond the now. We'll have to take her on her own terms. No questions, no answers. What happened in the time after leaving her baby in Florida and surfacing in the badlands of the West will stay under vigilant lock and key, as if her own existence depends on erasing the past. And maybe it does. Mama says Daddy misses her and wants both of us home for a visit this summer. Berta shuffles her feet and says she'll think about it. She's not sure she's ready. Whenever you are, darling, Mama says, whenever you are.

Then it's over. Everyone says good-bye and I'm on the bus again, rolling back up the coastline. The woman sitting next to me opens a bag of peanut butter and cheese crackers. She says she's retired and traveling to Orlando to see relatives.

"What about you, young lady?" She offers a snack. "Going to or coming back from somewhere?"

I stare at her for a moment. "Coming back," I say. "I've been visiting relatives too."

She nods, and I think I'm supposed to say more, but I just look out the window. I can't yet understand what it took for Berta to re-enter our world. She's come to us wrapped only in the strength that pulled her fingers around a pen and made words bleed onto a page that got folded into an envelope and dropped into the mouth of a mailbox somewhere in Arizona. I can't explain that this is why I'm here on this bus, at this moment. Something lightens inside me, just a little, and I turn to my traveling companion. "I was visiting my sister."

"That's nice."

"Yes," I say, "it was nice."

Chapter Twenty-Six

❄

Changes

"Hey, you!" Ellen Swisher waves me over at the end of math class at college. She has chestnut hair and a toothy smile. She hates math as much as I do. She gives a mock groan. "I'm glad that's over. Wanna grab some coffee?"

"Sure." My spirits lift when I'm with her; we're becoming friends. She reminds me of my roommate Beth at Howey. The next week she invites me to her house to study. She drives a blue Ford Falcon.

"Nice car," I say.

"Well, if you don't count the rust spots from the beach."

I didn't know you can drive on the sand here. She says I should come some weekend and we'll spend the whole day in

Cocoa Beach with her friends. I can hardly believe my good fortune. The Swishers live by the river in a house shaded by willows. Ellen's room is as happy as she is, with Beatles posters plastered on bright yellow walls. Like most men in this area, Mr. Swisher works for NASA at the Kennedy Space Center, and Ellen's mother is a schoolteacher. Her brothers are sixteen and fourteen, hefty and loud. After we finish our homework, Mrs. Swisher invites me to stay for dinner, but I say no, I have to get ready for work. Ellen drops me off at the apartment complex. I see the curtain in the apartment move as if someone has been watching from the inside. As I open the door, Denise's face is set in a sullen mold.

"Hi," I greet her as if everything is fine, which it should be, but of course it isn't. I'm home for dinner in plenty of time for our nightly ritual of eating mostly in silence, then me cleaning up and going to work at Sears. I take the bus now; it's safe enough, and besides, Ellen just got a part-time job in the Junior Department and she's volunteered to drive me home the nights our schedules match.

Denise just grunts and turns away. "What's the matter?" I ask as if I don't know she's jealous of anyone who wants to spend time with me.

"Nothing's wrong."

"Okay." I turn to enter my room and Denise slams the door to her bedroom. When Tom arrives she cranks up a smile and puts the spaghetti water on to boil. Tom opens a Pabst Blue Ribbon then flips the television dial while I set the table.

After our wordless dinner, I wash dishes and retreat to my room to write Berta. I'm still in some kind of limbo after the Miami reunion. I sort of have my sister back, but I don't, not really. We don't seem to be able to talk on the telephone without a lot of silences; maybe because I keep asking her questions she doesn't want to answer. I hint at how it would be fun to take a trip to Arizona when I save up enough money for train fare. Maybe someday, she says after a long pause. Sure.

So letter writing is safer. I'm not sure what we are to each other now—but we're not exactly friends. In time our letters get longer and I struggle to add pieces to the puzzle that is my sister. She's taking up motorcycle racing so she writes about rallies in places like Red Rock and Cave Creek. The family she lives with is related to some famous science fiction writer, so she's now reading books by Asimov, Bradbury, and other authors I've never heard of. She sends me a paperback copy of *Stranger in a Strange Land* by Robert Heinlein. I have trouble understanding the book but the title fits how I feel.

THE NEXT SUNDAY, a car honks once. It's Ellen; I've been ready for an hour. Denise and Tom have gone shopping for new stereo speakers. They wanted me to go with them, but I said I had other plans and Denise raise her eyebrows and said, "Oh?" As if nothing could be more fun than being with the two of them.

Ellen's Falcon whizzes over the causeway to Cocoa Beach and swings down a ramp onto a long strand of hard-packed sand. The beach is crammed with cars, families, teenagers, old men with fishing poles at water's edge, dogs chasing seagulls, and surfers riding the small waves. Ellen pulls up next to a turquoise Mustang convertible. A handsome boy in baggy shorts waves us over, one hand resting against a surfboard. The day is a haze of Coppertone #4 suntan oil, warm ocean water, and blasts of music from the car radio. We bake in the sun, splash in the waves, and get sand in everything. Ellen's friend Donny holds a bottle of suntan lotion like a microphone, screaming "Help!" along with The Beatles, and we laugh until we can hardly breathe.

At four o'clock we take a final rinse and Ellen drives me back to my apartment, radio blasting The Lovin' Spoonful's "Summer in the City." As I bounce up the stairs, I have a new feeling I can't quite place except that it feels like one of those times at Cocoloco when Daddy didn't drink and we fell asleep to tinkling rain after a good day. My cheeks ache from laughing and my body tingles with almost too much sun and a slick of coconut-scented lotion Ellen says will help cool the sunburn.

The good feelings dissipate when I open the door. I'm half an hour late for dinner, and I forgot to call Denise. She's waiting for me. I just stare as she storms and screams that I'm an inconsiderate bitch and look at everything she's done for me and the least I can do is show up on time. Tom raises his hand to calm her but she just wheels away, shouting, "You can make your own damn dinner!" I mumble I'm sorry and escape to my room. The next morning Denise is all normal again, smiling, showing me the new stereo system as she hands me a cup of coffee.

In math class Ellen says, "What's wrong with you? My gosh, you look like someone went and died on you."

I tell Ellen about Denise's fit and how it's been this way ever since I had to move in with her and Tom. She shakes her head.

"No one should treat you like that! Don't you see Denise is nuts?" It hasn't occurred to me that I might have a say in how I'm treated. After all, I explain to Ellen, it's because of Denise I have a room of my own and a roof over my head.

Ellen's jaw tightens and she looks at me like I'm the crazy one. "You don't understand, do you? That you deserve better?" I just look at her and shrug. I don't know if I can believe that.

Ellen invites me again to study at her house. When I arrive, Mrs. Swisher and the boys are waiting for me in the living room. Ellen says her mom has something she wants to ask me. I'm being invited to live with them until I finish junior college —if I'd like that. The Swishers are something I've never experienced: a real family, not like ours, even if Daddy always says we are a damn happy family. Tongue-tied, I nod yes, even though I'm scared about how Denise will take the news.

The next morning I head toward the kitchen, where Denise is pouring cereal into a bowl for Tom. My voice sticks in my throat and just a grunt comes out.

"Something wrong?"

This is what it would be like to face Daddy, I suddenly realize. That's why I'm so terrified. Denise isn't Daddy, I tell myself. Finally, the words squeak out, as if they've been strained through a metal sieve.

"I'm leaving. I mean—I'm moving out."

The words hang in the air, frozen. Tom clears his throat. Denise does a slow turn from the refrigerator and slams a bowl onto the counter. Her eyes spit fury. "You can't do this," she hisses through gritted teeth. "You *can't* leave." She turns to Tom for backup ammunition, but he doesn't take a shot. Instead, he just lifts his palms into the air.

"You can't stop her, Dee. It's a free country."

I'm buzzing with adrenaline, a hurricane swirling inside and threatening to turn my stomach inside out. I steady myself on the kitchen counter. It is the first time I've stood up to anyone, and so far it hasn't killed me. I can't look straight at Denise, so I glance at Tom, who gives me a small smile and starts fiddling with the salt and pepper shakers. *Click, click.*

Except for that sound, the room is silent. There's nothing left to say. The apartment feels airless, all sucked in on itself. I manage to pick up my feet and turn to the bedroom, wondering if a frying pan will fly through the air at my retreating back. Denise is still rooted in the same spot, glaring now at Tom. I pick up my key and walk two blocks to the nearest public telephone. I insert coins with trembling hands.

"I did it, Ellen. I did it." Now I sag with relief, shake off the storm clouds, and wince at how bright the sun is, the heat that's spreading through me like a balm. It all happens in a single afternoon, a blur of packing and Denise's grim face. In less than an hour the Falcon swings out of the driveway for the last time. The sign for the King Street Apartments—*Affordable Living on the Space Coast*—shrinks from sight. Finally, at nineteen going on twenty, I feel safe—and something like free.

The next Sunday I attend worship services with the whole family, taking my first step inside a Catholic church without being afraid of what Daddy would do if he found out. A guitarist leads a chorus of singers, and the stained glass windows cast brilliant sheets of color as the sun rises in the summer sky. I watch as the parishioners stand or kneel and perform their rituals. I don't go up to the altar for communion; that would be wrong, since I'm an impostor here, although I'm tempted to see if the silver cup holds wine or grape juice. I think about Daddy and all the years I was forbidden to enter Padre Daniel's church in Miches. During the final prayer, I bend too, knees resting on the worn wooden bar. I haven't been permitted to believe in God, and can't really see Him as an old white man in a fraying beard anyway. But here, as voices rise in prayer and the light bends rainbows onto our heads, I whisper, "*Thank you.*"

After church, Ellen and I fly away to the beach in the

Falcon. I'm soaring, a bird myself, skimming the ocean waves and landing softly on the salty sand. Later, back home with my new family, Mr. Swisher fires up the charcoal grill to barbecue steaks. Ellen and I strip corn from stalks and wrap them in foil with butter and salt and pepper, lining them up like silver presents around the edges of the grill. The boys, complaining mildly, make a salad of tomatoes and iceberg lettuce. We chatter, laugh, and eat at the picnic table under the shade tree as the sun sets, in the magic time before the mosquitoes show up. No awkward silences here. A wedge of watermelon and a plate of brownies appear. Sated and sticky with watermelon, I sigh in disbelief. For the first time I have the American family I used to dream of—and a best friend, too. Slowly the ever-present knots in my stomach loosen and I feel like I can breathe without taking in jagged breaths. I'm smoothing out somehow.

I've saved up enough money to buy my first car. I hand over four hundred dollars to a friend of Donny's and become the owner of a 1961 white Oldsmobile F85 with glasspacks, whatever that means. What it means, I find out, is a very loud muffler that impresses the Swisher boys, and a car I can accelerate up to 110 miles per hour on the long stretch between Cocoa and Daytona Beach, which I don't tell anyone about. Eventually the muffler falls off and I replace it with a regular type, which disappoints Ellen's brothers immensely.

Just as the car is expanding my actual horizons, the Swishers gradually push me further into other worlds into which I've never dared venture. In the few months I've been with them, cracks and deep fissures have appeared in my body armor, though the dark fog of fear that lives inside is still there. There's room now, for the first time, for something else. In listening to Ellen and her parents, I learn that it's okay to question, to ask, to wonder about almost anything. They discuss what jobs Ellen and I might be able to get once we've finished with junior college. Mrs. Swisher hastens to add, that is, unless either of us plans to get our bachelor's degree. As if we actually do have choices. Mr. Swisher says there are hundreds of jobs opening up at Cape Kennedy what with the Apollo-Saturn projects and the race to land a man on the moon. My head spins with excitement, and I tell the other voice, that one that says *"No, you'll never be good enough to do any of this,"* to shut up.

I buy a flowered notebook with a tiny lock. Inside, I write: "A Plan for 1967"—for next year. The blank page stares at me, and the fog settles in. It feels dangerous and too daring to write down actual words, plans for the future. Instead, I tuck the blank diary under my pillow. A few stray thoughts linger like wispy breezes. I close my eyes and let myself dream that I have my very own apartment, just for me. It's tidy and shipshape, bright and filled with friends on weekends. I imagine that during the week I'll drive over the Merritt Island causeway to Cape Kennedy, where I'll be waved into a tall building humming with scientists and the thrill of space travel.

I feel brave enough to call Berta again to see if she's ready for a visit home. This time she doesn't hesitate too long before saying yes. We make plans to fly to the Dominican Republic in December, after both the hurricane season and the political turbulence in Santo Domingo have simmered down enough for travel. It will be Berta's first trip back since she was forced by Daddy to leave Miches that pregnant summer seven long years ago.

I guess Berta is finally ready to face Daddy, but now the long-ago fog settles back into my stomach as if it never went away. I hug a pillow and breathe slowly. The heaviness lifts a little, but I'm not sure if I'm ready for whatever fireworks await on the island.

I'm only now putting together the pieces of myself, patching the cracks and creating something that's almost whole. We've been blown apart for so long, I'm afraid what another explosion will do to me—and to the rest of the family.

Chapter Twenty-Seven

※

Homecoming

Mama and Daddy won't be meeting us at the airport. Daddy, it seems, has been stricken harder than usual with *gripe* and is still recovering. I wonder if he's really been sick at all. He's never apologized for anything he said to Berta that horrible summer or about her in the years after. The night before our flight home, Berta and I meet at the same Miami hotel where we stayed with Mama and Aunt Betty in April. Her hair isn't all stiff and sprayed up any more. It's loose and pretty and ripples against her shoulders. That is the only thing that's flowing easily. Her back is hunched as if for battle, she's bitten her fingernails until they bleed, and even as we talk, she picks at her lips. My stomach is all bunched up, wondering and worrying how it's going to be with Daddy.

"You excited?" I ask after we're settled in the booth of the hotel coffee shop, aware this is a stupid question. *Terrified* would be the proper response.

"It will be nice to see everyone again," she answers in an even tone, looking at the menu.

"Oh, come on."

"My friends, I mean."

The waitress takes our orders for tuna sandwiches and iced tea.

"What about Daddy?'

Her tone gets sharp. "That's up to him."

I don't know what else to say, or how to have a conversation. We eat our food and make small talk about movies and books. We share a slice of key lime pie that is so tangy Berta makes a funny face, and we both laugh. It feels odd not to have the kinds of intimate talks with her that I have with Ellen, but I figure we're just getting used to each other. Berta's twenty-four and I'm twenty, all grown up but almost as scared as we were when we were children waiting for nighttime and the sound of rum being poured over ice.

Layers of Spanish and English babble over the loud-speakers near the Dominicana Airlines counter. Christmas ornaments and garlands frame the departure gates. Bright red, green, blue, and yellow colors shimmer in the long line to the ticket counter as colorfully dressed Dominicans going home for the holidays push huge boxes, bundles, and suitcases along in front of them. The shifting sea of travelers flows around the obstacles like a tide, and no one seems to mind the queue. Laughter and chatter surround us as we join the throng. We stand out like tall, pale ghosts in our sensible traveling skirts and small suitcases. Berta still uses the old white bag with a brocade pattern, now scuffed and dulled to gray.

I see an old sparkle in Berta's eyes. She puts her fingers to her lips and I nod. We've both realized none of these people can guess we speak Spanish. It's like when we were young and visiting the capital. We'd eavesdrop as everyone talked around us, never knowing that we understood every word. We'd keep up the pretense except for the few times when boys would say things about us that they'd never dare say out loud in front of Dominican girls. If no grownups were around we'd turn back to these hecklers and spew out a river of colorful Miches curses. The boys would stop dead in their tracks, mouths open in embarrassment and shock. Before they could respond, we'd spin around and walk away tall with dignity, still looking—to them, at least—just like foreign tourists. When they were out of earshot, we'd double over in laughter.

Once aloft, we both settle into our own thoughts. I have so much I want to say, to ask my sister-stranger, but the hum of the aircraft and the splatter of conversations are comforting, a welcome blanket over my anxious mind. Berta pulls out a paper sack crammed with a book, magazines, and articles she's torn out of newspapers.

"You travel prepared, huh?"

"Well, sure. We have hours to kill. Need something to read?"

"I guess."

She rummages around and shows me an article on forest preservation she's cut out of some magazine. I shake my head no. "Here's something you probably haven't seen for a long time. I was going through some papers and found Daddy's opus."

"Daddy's what?"

"You remember that article he wrote ages ago that he thought *National Geographic* would print? We always called it Daddy's opus."

I say maybe I'll remember it if I read it again. She pulls out a thick sheaf of papers from a long envelope and hands it to me, saying, "Yeah, if you read this, you'd think we had just a wonderful life in Miches. Well, Daddy, anyway. We're hardly mentioned at all. But then again, what would we expect, right?"

"Right."

I spread open the tissue-thin sheets of paper, and now I remember the months that Daddy—in the mornings, sober of course—would take a lined notebook with him when he fired up the furnace in the drying shed at Cocoloco. He'd bring his completed pages to Mama so she could type his notes up on the Royal typewriter. Her typing is as fast as rain hammering on the roof. His story was never published, but he sent copies to friends in the States curious about our strange life. I read aloud some of what Daddy wrote in 1958 about Miches:

> *Six years ago a number of coconut palms coming into production persuaded us to move here, bag and baggage, plus our daughters Berta and Rita. There is a local expression that "el ojo del amo engorda el caballo" which means the owner's eye fattens the horse, and I wanted to get started on personal management of the finca. After all, I had to start learning about coconut growing sometime, as my past experience in farming had been limited to kitchen gardens of radishes, tomatoes and the like. At long last, Cocoloco finca is beginning to prove itself not so "loco."*
>
> *There is not much social life in Miches, but with friends and the bright lights of the capital only three hours away by car it is*

not missed. (Perhaps it is just as well there isn't too much activity because Emily has very nicely managed to teach the children, by means of the Calvert correspondence courses.)

BERTA INTERRUPTS. "Oh, sure, only three hours away to the excitement of the capital. As if we ever got out of Miches more than once a year."

I skim past all the descriptions of Cocoloco and how the plantation runs until I get to the part of about the *velorios*, the ancient drumming ceremonies that happened every June. I'd forgotten about them. Now I remember Padre Daniel once said that *velorios* were the work of the devil. Berta stares out the airplane window as I read aloud. Seeing Daddy's words, I remember the hot June nights, lying in bed to the throb of drums, which rose and fell like waves. Even the frogs and crickets seemed to stop and listen to the ancient sounds of drums and voodoo. The stewardess brings cups of ginger ale and packets of peanuts. I put away Daddy's story, then pull out the last page and decide to read his final sentence. "Listen to this," I say to Berta:

"We have had our trials and tribulations, and expect more before our plans and hopes are realized, but as the steamship companies advertise—'getting there is half the fun.'"

Berta sniffs at that. "Oh yeah, getting there was definitely half the fun, all right." Her voice, sarcastic and bitter, makes me feel oddly defensive of Daddy. Maybe I have this reaction because of all the years she missed; the times that weren't so bad, except when they were. Sadness seeps in like a mist after reading Daddy's words. It's all true, what he writes, but it's as if there's another person on these pages, another Daddy—not the rum-crazed father who yanks us out of safe beds on dark nights and makes Mama cry.

Berta is dry-eyed when we land, wearing her sorrow like a shield, and soon we're on the familiar cross-island journey. The driver says that the main road over the mountain is impassable; we won't get to stop at the top of the mountain ridge for the ritual of seeing Cocoloco like we're used to on every trip home. My heart sinks at the news. Here was the one place we could see Daddy's entire dream come true, the swath of coconut fronds next to the beach, nestled right up to the turquoise bay. Our world, our life—growing and glowing off in the distance, always beautiful. Sometimes this sight even seemed to make everything worthwhile.

Instead, we detour away, turning into unknown hills and passing papaya trees swollen with fruit, straggly settlements too small to be called villages, and stands of coffee trees with their bright red berries. It begins to rain, and the sweet smells of wet earth and cool rain engulf the car. I take a big gulp of wet air, and almost as swiftly as it began, the rain stops, and a double rainbow appears then disappears. We get stuck in one rut for almost half an hour before the driver and two men riding donkeys manage to yank the car out and back on somewhat solid ground. This is unfamiliar territory, so we're both startled when, after another hour of lurches and turns, we suddenly arrive in Miches. Berta squeezes my arm so tightly it stings as our eyes strain in the dusk.

The driver pulls up to the gate at Casalata and honks his horn. We spill out of the car, try to shake off the ghosts of the past, and brace ourselves for the unknown. The gate is locked, but there's no need to ring the bell. Mama's small shape hurries toward us, her steps jerky and fast. Daddy, rigid as a soldier, marches behind. It's too far away to see his eyes or smell for liquor. I've forgotten to tell Berta how Daddy has aged; I've forgotten to warn her how small everything will seem. I've forgotten to tell her he isn't as scary as he used to be. Too late now. I can't tell her everything, and she won't tell me anything. We stand together and I feel her tremble, her skin cold and clammy in the warm evening.

"Girls—you're really here!" Mama's voice cracks as she fumbles with the lock. Daddy's arms don't seem to know what to do; they jerk and twitch, and his mouth opens and closes, trying but failing to speak. For a few seconds we're all frozen in our tracks and I can feel the numbness seep in, that fog I pull around me for protection from danger or at least the anticipation of something bad. A cough behind me from the driver, and the silence is broken. He's waiting to be paid.

"*Un momento*," Daddy says, and then his arms reach out toward us, and I step aside so it's just Berta in front of him. They face each other. She straightens up so she's almost as tall as he is.

"How are you?" he asks.

"Fine."

I feel faint and realize I've been holding my breath. Mama's hand finds mine. It's damp with perspiration. A frog croaks off in the distance, and a mosquito buzzes against my cheek. In the corner of my vision, the driver has backed away to give us privacy. He leans against the hood of his car and turns his head to light a cigarette. The smoke curls around his fingers and a red dot glows in the shadowy dusk.

"Well," Daddy says. "Well."

Berta remains still. I can tell she's not going to make any

move. *I'm here*, says her straight spine. *I'm here*, say her clenched fists. *It's your turn*, says her jaw, thrust forward. *Your turn*, says her blue stare. A strangled groan rises from Daddy's throat, and then he's reaching, reaching, crying. Berta lets him hold her, lets him pull her in, lets him sob into her pretty hair. She's still tight and stiff, not ready for any kind of surrender, not now. By the looks of it, maybe never. Mama is crying now, long gasping mews. She pulls me with her and we join in the awkward hug. I stay safe in my fog. I sniff the air like a dog but I don't smell rum, just exhaustion, fear, relief, and adrenaline. Daddy steps back and composes himself. He pulls out some bills from his worn khaki shorts and finds the driver.

"*Ay, que bueno*," says the driver, not to the money but to the family, together again. "*Hace mucho tiempo, sí?*" he asks. It's been a long time, yes?

"*Sí, demasiado.*" Yes, too long, Daddy answers. Too long.

On our first night together again, we are like swimmers just trying to stay afloat on the sea. Beneath us, the ocean of our life heaves and groans with the weight of everything that's unsaid and will remain unsaid. This sea is all churned up and monsters lurk in its depths, the events and facts of which we must not speak. Sharks hide in the shallows, moray eels slip through forests of kelp, ready to nip if we sink. So we flail about on the surface to keep from bumping too close to each other. Yet we are afloat, all of us finally here in one place, together.

I close my eyes and get sucked down in the undertow of an unwanted image. That's where she is, that other girl, the one who really was murdered and tossed into the Gulf. The one we thought was Berta. I don't know why I have to think of her now. I've never even thought of her family before, whoever they are, wherever they live. Or was she all alone, with no one to ever miss her? I beat my way back up to the surface, paddling my legs as hard as I can.

We skim our conversations off the top like fishermen flinging nets to catch the fish that swim close to the surface. Daddy says we've got a bumper crop of nuts but the price is dropping. Juan Kair's son found a gold nugget in the river near La Mina and they displayed it in the store until a thief broke in and stole it. Two new bars have opened up in the hills behind the baseball field. Mama says there's a new medical clinic in town, and a dentist who splits his time between El Seybo and Miches, not like in the old days when we'd have to wait weeks with a toothache or travel all the way to the capital. I describe my new life with the Swishers, but I don't tell them how they are the family I've always wanted. I tell them Ellen and I plan to get jobs at NASA next year, and maybe our own apartment. Mama says "Oh my goodness, that sounds so grand. Keep up the typing."

Berta says she might move to California in a couple of years when she can afford it. Mama heats up beans and cooks a pot of rice. Daddy sips his rum and coughs a lot, but says he's getting better. The *gripe* had a good grip on him, he jokes. Berta produces a tight little smile. Mama has cleaned out the storage boxes from our bedroom and made up the beds with clean sheets and new mosquito netting.

Berta and I trip over each other unpacking in the tiny space between the beds. She opens the window to the night. A faint breeze sifts through the heavy tension. The early evening quiet is shattered by radios blasting holiday songs. Daddy pulls out the old Victrola and plays Perry Como's Christmas album, which muffles the outside noise somewhat. Before supper we pour ourselves tall glasses of Presidente beer and sit on the porch with Mama and Daddy. Berta's jaw relaxes a notch, so I do too.

Without warning, the lights go out and all noise drops to a sigh. The darkness is softened by a quarter moon and a paradise of stars. The four of us walk out to the front gate and look over the harbor. Here and there flickers of light appear, like fireflies glowing, as kerosene lanterns are lit. Just like when we were small, before power came to Miches. We don't talk. With no radios to blare, no motors, generators, or other noise, we hear the slap of waves breaking, palm fronds whispering high above our heads, and the occasional screech of crickets.

We eat by lantern light, which casts a honey glow. An illusion of coziness, we're a surreal version of a Norman Rockwell painting, napkins tucked in and lamplight glinting gold off our glasses. Daddy has stayed moderately sober, which is enough to cheer me up. We sit in our seats just like the old days, as if nothing much has changed except Berta and I got bigger and Mama and Daddy got smaller and the house has shrunk too.

Daddy lifts his glass in a toast. "To our happy family." Berta chokes on her beer. I gulp mine down in one big swig, and then say "Amen" before bursting out with a hysterical cackle. Berta kicks my leg under the table and then tries to stifle a chuckle. Mama looks puzzled, but she and Daddy start to laugh anyway, until the aluminum walls reverberate with the unfamiliar sound. Beyond the *laguna*, the frogs fall silent and even the crickets quiet down.

Daddy told me years ago that the eye of a hurricane has the lowest sea-level atmospheric pressure on earth. The eye can range from a few kilometers to over a hundred miles across. The calm is deceiving, of course—but for its duration, it's a time to draw some full breaths, to take a break and prepare before being lashed again by the wall of the storm. Cocoloco is the eye of the hurricane, the place where for a few precious days we rest, a family united by a cyclone of secrets and lies and a bud of hope that we'll somehow weather the storms that surround us. In its center we knit a peace, a fragile blanket as thin as a spider's web. We stitch it with careful words, with no words. Daddy hardly drinks for the entire visit; his sober nights are woven into this blanket too. So are the still-awkward hugs, and the evenings we play four rounds of Scrabble and it doesn't matter who wins. For two weeks we huddle in the center. Here in the eye the winds are slight and patches of blue sky freckle the bay with clear winter light.

On our last night a rain shower taps its way across our roof, light at first, then letting loose like a pounding drum. I lean over and shake Berta awake.

"Listen," I whisper. She sits up as the rain slanting in the open window sprinkles the mosquito netting with raindrops like pearls in the dim light.

"Let's go outside," Berta murmurs.

"Now?"

"Yes, now."

"Why?"

"I don't know. The rain will feel good."

We tiptoe outside in our pajamas, feet squishing in the wet grass. Berta puts her face up to the rain and opens her mouth. Like a little girl, I stick my tongue out to catch the drops as they slide down off my nose. Berta giggles, and I say "Shhh."

"Oh, they can't hear anything with this downpour."

When we start to get soaked, we duck under the roof and perch on the porch step to dry off. As the squall passes, the moon slips out from behind the clouds and the stars are freshly washed diamonds.

"Look." Berta points down to the step.

"What?"

"Remember? Our feet." I'd forgotten that when Casalata was built, Daddy and Mama had a special ceremony to mark its completion. Daddy mixed the concrete himself for the last job —the porch step that leads to the *laguna*. Berta and I got to leave our footprints in the drying cement. Water has puddled in the shallow indentations, making them stand out in the light of the moon.

We sit together and stare off into our own galaxies. I pat my tiny footprints as if they're flesh and blood, still part of that five-year-old child who pressed her feet into the cool gray cement so long ago. I run my fingers over my sister's larger prints. My heart feels tender and raw. A cloud drifts over the moon and reminds me of the darkness of hurricanes. Even if a big one comes, bigger than Casalata can stand, these footprints will survive. Berta slips her arm over my shoulder, her skin sticky with goose bumps but comforting anyway. I jump at the unexpected tenderness. Her eyes drop their shields and for just a moment she lets me see all the way through the dark blue night of her pain, and out beyond to the wheeling stars where everything is all right, all the time.

Epilogue

Chapter Twenty-Eight

❋

Suitcase, California

Deep in the dim light of Berta's hall closet, hidden by old coats and blankets, I find the suitcase. Its battered white plastic has a molded brocade pattern, now weathered after decades of journeys. This is its final resting place. My heart races. Is it locked? Holding my breath, I slide the snaps, and they pop right open with that satisfying *snark* sound—decisive and loud. A musty smell engulfs me, filling the space with the stale aroma of old secrets. Inside, the ice-blue satin lining has come unglued, and the gathered pockets at the sides and back gape open in a collective yawn. The sagging elastic gave up trying to keep anything secure long ago.

She bought the luggage when she was still a teenager, that

first year she left the island to attend boarding school in the States. She lugged it with her for over forty years, starting from our home in the Dominican Republic. It traveled first to the high school in Florida, where she disappeared. It was almost six years later when she and it emerged into the hot sun of Arizona, as suddenly as she had vanished. Even with this miracle—the shock and joy of her resurrection—my sister's determined silence lasted her entire lifetime. It was clear: I was not to pry, ever. Now here I am, doing just that. Guilt and shame battle with a hungry need to know. My throat is dry and my hands tremble. This container of her past is filled with small and large envelopes, photographs, bulging bundles of papers once held together by rubber bands that have grown limp and are now stuck to them like strands of overcooked spaghetti.

I sit back heavily on the floor and hold my sister's life in my arms. Will it tell me who she is, who she was, beyond the little she revealed about the gaping hole in her life?

Someone wrote that "death is the ultimate invasion of privacy," or words to that effect. I think of this as I begin to excavate, to hunt for what I do not know. A thick paper bag is crammed with small notebooks. So this is where she stored her years, in tiny Hallmark calendars with inch-square spaces for each day. Small, dry facts shorthand their way across the page. I flip the doll-sized booklet back to her birthday in 1968 and read: *Civil service exam. Nap. Cleaned.*

I find a large stack of photographs, the ones she kept through more than half a century: There's a black-and-white picture of our grandmother, looking dignified against the banister of her Southampton home. Here's a photo of our family posing in front of a young palm on a deserted stretch of beach, probably taken on our first trip to Miches. Daddy is holding Berta's hand. She's four, pulling away and squinting uncertainly into the sun. I'm just a baby, nestled in Mama's arms. My parents are smiling, eyes bright with adventure and promise. I don't remember them like this. I set the picture aside, that window into hope and possibility, careful to smooth out the tattered edges. Next I pull out snapshots and awkward notes I sent to my sister that first year we communicated by mail, oh-so-gingerly, after her reappearance.

A series of photographs from a later time spill out from a torn envelope—nudes, obviously taken by a lover. In them, she peeks out from behind a waterfall of hair, eyes smiling at the photographer. They must have been taken after she moved to California. She's sitting on river rocks, her long blonde mane cascading over her breasts and eddying around her knees. She looks happy. She didn't cut her hair for more than thirty years. I still remember her asking me to go with her for a haircut, decades later, when she was in her late forties. It took her this long to allow a change. She didn't want to go to the hairdresser alone, my sister who by now was traveling the world by herself, working hard jobs as a forest ranger or park ranger and collecting books and friends with equal enthusiasm. I was grateful she needed me that day when she shed her mane of protection, although even then she couldn't let it go entirely. In the pocket of a manila folder, I find the ponytail of blond hair curled up like a sleeping snake. Tied in a blue ribbon, it's almost two feet long.

The contents of this suitcase represent everything that was valuable to her, so I'm still hoping I'll learn about the years of which I was never to speak. But the suitcase mocks me in the end. If I want to know exactly what she did on a particular day, six years ago, twenty-five years ago, I can find her scribbled notes. But she keeps that other time secret, even to herself—and now she's gone, taken by cancer at age sixty. The light outside has faded into dusk and I'm still sitting on the floor. Finally I close the suitcase—there's no more I will know. The house is cleaned out now; there is nothing else to find. Instead, I must focus on what has been revealed by these carefully hidden bundles. Even if she had to abandon us for those long and aching years, she protected what mattered, and kept us safe with her all along.

TODAY IS THE FOURTH OF JULY. I reach up to the top of the bookcase for a velvet-wrapped box. I think I should be doing this with more ceremony—that I should be dressed up, not wearing a torn T-shirt. I untie the gold cord and pull out a heavy gray box sealed with a cross of white packing tape. I wonder if it will be as hard to open as Mama's container was after her death. Berta and I had to wrestle that lid off with a screwdriver and hammer. But I rip off the tape, and the cover yields instantly to my touch. Inside, a plastic bag is tied off with a twist-tie, the kind we use at a grocery store.

The bag has taken the shape of the container, like a brick of clay ready to be molded into a new creation. It is said that your ashes are the same weight as you when you're born. I don't know if that's true, but it sags into the curve of my arm. The line from a song comes into mind and I change it slightly: *She's not heavy; she's my sister.* I place my cargo into a daypack and step out into the early morning. I'm taking Berta to the park where she worked for almost twenty years. I know she'd rather be there as the quiet cove wakes up to the ducks and seagulls, the joggers, walkers, and today, the many picnickers who will swarm in later with their coolers and charcoal and ribs.

The sun glints on the tops of skyscrapers across the bay, and a bank of gray fog hovers low along the waterfront. I crunch across the gravel path to the fresh trail at the edge of the inlet. A section of recently acquired marshland is still fenced off, growing wild with weeds and poison oak. A sign says "*AREA CLOSED—do not enter until it has been made accessible and safe for the public.*" Several small pines, gangly as teenagers, are just ahead. I kneel into the damp grass next to the smallest sapling, which glistens with dew, its branches as tender as dawn. I study the footpath and for the moment no one is in sight. On bent knee I rip open the plastic and pour handfuls of ashes around the base of the pine. I run my hands through my sister's remains, blending them into the surrounding earth, and my fingers turn silver and gritty. A group of walkers is nearing, so I slip away as nonchalantly as possible.

The pond in the middle of the park is still in the soft light. A loon bobs and dives, leaving circles that fan out slowly then quiet to stillness again. I wait until the strollers are far beyond the curve of the trail, then pour a stream of gray into the pond. It blooms into a whitish cloud underwater, spreading in swirls of light and shadow. Berta loved the water almost as much as her job. She's part of it now, swimming in millions of specks among the reeds in the sun-warmed shallows.

Thirty-one years ago it was Mama and Berta and me standing on a cliff at the edge of the Pacific Ocean in Mexico, casting Daddy's ashes to the water below. After discovering that Daddy's lingering *gripe* was really lung cancer, they sold the *finca* and moved to Mexico for his final years, leaving most of their belongings for the new owner of Casalata. Anything too treasured to bear a stranger's touch they threw into the *laguna*. I can see it all falling, sinking as my own heart sinks, tumbling into the dark waters. The odd sparkle of a gem, my paintings, family photographs, notes typed on the old Royal, double-spaced on onionskin paper—scraps of a life and a family beached on a deceptively gentle shore. The typewriter itself, plummeting beneath the layers of the *laguna*, scattering tadpoles and turtles and dreams in its path.

I shake myself back to the present but the past swirls around and now I'm remembering the Tijuana hospital and Daddy swaddled in white sheets, thin brown arms hooked to IVs and tubes. When he sees us he opens his mouth in a toothless grimace that tries to be a smile. We make small talk, the kind you make when you can't say what's really happening so it doesn't happen. When we step outside for a break, Daddy rests his head back into the pillow. "See you later, alligator."

"After awhile, crocodile," I manage through the lump in my throat.

We come back inside the room and minutes later Mama jumps up and her cry lies there in the still air and we move quietly, as if silence matters—but it doesn't anymore. When we spread his ashes, the wind spins them around and coats us all with shards of bone. We don't know what to do so we laugh uneasily as we shake Daddy from our hair and clothing. Maybe he doesn't want to leave us, I say.

YEARS AFTER OUR FATHER'S DEATH, Mama moved here to be near us and adopted the park as her own. She took her walks here every morning without fail, unless it was raining heavily, always carrying a spare plastic bag to scoop up any discarded trash on the trail. Mama lived until she was ninety-one, and was healthy almost up to the end. Five years ago, Berta and I spread her ashes under a young bush full of glossy leaves. The bush has since grown strong and thick with foliage and is beginning to look like a tree; we call it Mama's tree. And now here I am, this time alone, spreading the last bit of Berta's ashes to join Mama in a light snowfall around the trunk. Now it's Berta's tree, too.

I put the now-empty bag in one of the trash cans. Sometime later today, one of Berta's former work companions will empty the can, not knowing what they're lifting into the park truck she used to drive. My legs give way and I crumple into a park bench. A seagull cocks his head at me a few feet away. The morning wakes up around me and the sun climbs higher. A slight breeze riffles the surface into points of light. I pull myself heavily off the bench and head home, passing the sign again, the one that says "*AREA CLOSED.*"

Berta had areas of her life that were always closed, that never felt safe enough to open for public access, even to me. But it's Independence Day, and today she's finally free. It dawns on me that I now have the liberty to open up to the deep place where the secrets have remained hidden and tearing me up inside for so long. *It's not too late*, I tell myself, even as something akin to fear courses through my body, but maybe it's not fear at all. Maybe I don't know what real hope and freedom feels like.

Chapter Twenty-Nine

✳

Palm Song

Despite once vowing to never return to this island, I am here once again. On the bus trip over the mountain, I ask the driver to pull over at the summit when the crescent of Samana Bay comes into view. He remembers me from when I was little. "*Sí, sí, por seguro.*" Of course I'll stop. He opens the door and gestures at the long sweep of palm groves at the edge of the turquoise water below, as if I wouldn't remember where to look—as if this precious view weren't seared into my soul. I shade my eyes to see if Cocoloco still stands out from the rest of the *fincas* like it did when our coconut trees were young and the fronds were a lighter green than the other palms in neighboring farms. But the *finca* blends in now with the rest, boundaries and color blurred by time and age. I close my eyes and Daddy is pulling my five-year-old self up onto a rock for a better view. But I don't need him this time; I still know where to look, what exact curve of beach draws me back.

My feet dig into wet Cocoloco sand as stories in my head fade in and out like the stations on the old Zenith radio, once our only link to an outside world. A memory pushes in from a few years ago, when my mother's life was waning. I asked her if she'd ever jotted down an outline of our family's many journeys —something I could hang my memories onto before they faded forever. She stiffened and a hard tone filtered through her voice, a smoky ember that choked her words.

"I wrote a book about our family once, you know."

"You did? What happened to it?"

She shrugged, her voice now a dying spark, all the fire drained away. "Your father didn't think much of it, and you children weren't particularly interested in your past. I threw it away."

So I've returned to this beach, standing unsteadily as ghosts spin in the warm breath of the trade winds. A green coconut bobs in the surf a few yards away. It will eventually drift ashore and sprout, much as we did, or tried to. I squint at the sun through tears. I remember those spurts of time when my sister and I were children, when laughter lit up our life, before the numbness set in like fog. Other memories flood in, unwanted, and ebb like the tide. I think of Luís and wonder what happened to him. I heard he married and is a grandfather now. I lean against the aged trunk of a palm, pockmarked with beetle holes and scarred by hurricanes. Planted ages ago by my father, the trunk still pushes skyward, its topknot tattered but still bearing fruit. It drops a ripe nut a few yards away, scattering a few sand crabs. The breeze freshens and the coconut grove becomes a loud chorus.

A short distance away the river beckons, its caramel surface dammed up by a sand bar. The water dims to dark red at its depths. It is deceptively still, hiding sodden logs and branches ripped from its banks when the rains caused the river to swell. Now the storms have passed and the river has settled back on itself, making a lagoon. The beach is empty except for a lone horse and rider ambling past at the water's edge. The man whistles a low tune and his saddlebags, filled with husked coconuts, sway from side to side. They don't see me, a ghost in the blue shadows of the riverbank.

I've walked here from the *finca* house a half a kilometer away. Its original skeleton is intact even now. The owner who bought our property over four decades ago has left some things unchanged still, like the Adirondack chairs, still painted turquoise, and the picnic table with the faint cigarette burn marks. The downstairs, which used to be open, is screened in now, and another room has been added, along with a sturdy water tower to catch rainfall. It's as if Daddy's pulse still beats inside, but it's no longer as open to the elements or to the unknown. It's encased, grown more solid, unyielding.

In many ways I'm like that house, sealed by the hard casings that grew over my core and tried to keep me from too much pain those early years. I know about protection; it's the same shell that also kept me from ever saying yes to bright-eyed men who dreamed of babies and who asked me to be their partner. But I'm melting despite myself, yielding to this beach, as Daddy did when he gave his heart to the trade winds, to the dance of sunlight on blue water. He gave us this long stretch of sand to play on, to dream on. He gave us fireflies and skies full of stars.

We were the rhythm of *merengue*, and the taste of *dulce de coco*. He gave us *chubascos*, those swift rainstorms that thundered down on Casalata like heaven's fury, and hurricanes, too. So we grew like weeds in this sweet wildness, burnt by the sun, blown away by Daddy's storms, and yet, like seeds, reborn again.

Here, in this place that is no longer home but which still holds me fast, sadness and loss make way for something else. I tremble and let the music of the palm trees sing its way into that dark place, let it begin to thaw. I pick up a twig and trace a shallow canal through the top of the sand bar. A trickle of water leaks into the fissure, then stops. I dig deeper, and it fills some more. I tunnel harder, until sweat drips off my nose, and watch as the water starts flowing of its own accord, telling its story as it plows through melting sand and finds a steady path to the mother ocean.

Author's Note

It is not easy to write about a family submerged in secrets, nor to expose truths long buried. The best any of us can do is to rely on memory, which shape-shifts as we grow older but is our only truth nevertheless. This book involves family members who have died, and people with whom I've not had contact for many decades. To honor and respect their privacy, I have changed some names and other personal details. In some cases I compressed or expanded time for better narrative continuity, but the events described in this book are otherwise factually accurate.

Captions

※

Acknowledgments

I come from a family of voracious readers and would-be writers. As a child, I wrote constantly and secretly, and words along with painting and drawing, became my lifeboat and refuge. My father wrote a never-published article about our adventures in the Dominican Republic. My mother wrote her own manuscript on that subject and discarded it after apparent indifference from her husband and children, although I never remember seeing it at all. I need to thank my mother, whose primary wish for me was that I become proficient in typing and shorthand so I could work as a secretary. Thankfully, knowing how to type has had other benefits as well.

A chance decision to take an essay workshop from Thom Elkjer resulted in my first published piece and the introduction to the camaraderie and magic of writing groups. Thank you to so many of my fellow-journeyers: Kaye McKinzie, Donna Emerson, Barbara Euser, Gregg Elliott, Laurie Oman, Paula Terrey, Marianne Manilov, Marianna Cacciatore, and more. A note of gratitude to Book Passage and Leslie Keenan's classes. Thanks also to Hedgebrook's "Writers in Residence" Program, a sanctuary where I turned scattered notes into the beginnings of a memoir and myself into a writer. I also appreciate all my friends who have patiently read various drafts along the way.

Thank you to Brooke Warner and She Writes Press for publishing this book. I owe a debt of gratitude to Liz Kracht, who edited my work vigorously and helped me to understand what language sings and what plods along, begging to be cut. I must also thank my childhood friends from the Dominican

Republic, who lived through extreme political turmoil in their country but never lost their love for home. This book could never have been written if, so many decades ago, *Michero* hearts hadn't opened wide to embrace an *extranjero* family into their lives and community. *Gracias, mis amigos de siempre.*

Reader's Guide

QUESTIONS FOR DISCUSSION

1. What made you want to read this book and suggest it for discussion?

2. What do you think motivated the author to share her life story? What was your response to her voice?

3. What do you think the significance of the title *The Coconut Latitudes* is?

4. Is this an end-of-an-era story about a family saga, or a story about the author learning to love her family and herself, despite traumatic events?

5. Discuss the importance of place in this memoir. How does the author use the contrast between life in the Dominican Republic and life in America as a tool?

6. One of the questions this book asks is about the importance of truth and honesty in family relationships, and about acceptance and forgiveness, especially in the relationship to self. Discuss how this is explored in the memoir.

7. In what ways do different kinds of love help Rita to reflect on her life throughout the memoir? Her ties with her sister, mother, and father, before and after their deaths? Her relationship with her childhood dog, and her friendships as a teen? Her love of art, travel, and writing?

8. How does Rita's relationship with her family change during her last visit home?

9. What do you think most inspires Rita's final reckoning with family events when she visits the place of her childhood? Her age, the need to let the past and its mysteries go, her role as survivor and keeper of secrets? How is her decision-making process different in later life than it is in her early twenties?

10. A shared love for their life in the Dominican Republic binds Rita and her sister together as children. Do you think that Rita's need to know Berta's secret about her disappearance limits their relationship as adult siblings?

11. Discuss how the need for a creative and authentic life leads Rita to the life transition central to her memoir. What other life events do you think form or sustain a person's sense of meaning in adult life when they have been marked by a childhood trauma?

12. How did your view of each of the characters change as you read the book?

13. Discuss the book's structure and the author's use of language and writing style. How does she draw the reader in and keep the reader engaged? Does she convey her story with insight, acceptance, self-pity, or something else?

14. Compare this book to other memoirs your group has read. Is it similar to any of them? What do you think your lasting impression of the book will be?

About the Author

RITA GARDNER grew up on her expatriate family's coconut farm in the Dominican Republic during the dictatorship of Rafael Trujillo. Living in a remote coastal village, she was home-schooled and began reading, writing, and painting at a young age. She went to Florida to finish school and later moved to the Bay Area in Northern California, where she follows her passions: trail hiking, traveling, writing, and photography. Her published essays, articles, and poems have appeared in literary journals, travel magazines, and newspapers. Her photographs show in galleries and other venues. She continues to dream in Spanish, dance the *merengue*, and gather inspiration from the ocean; her favorite color is Caribbean blue.

SELECTED TITLES FROM SHE WRITES PRESS

She Writes Press is an independent publishing company
founded to serve women writers everywhere.
Visit us at www.shewritespress.com.

*Don't Call Me Mother: A Daughter's Journey from Abandonment to
Forgiveness* by Linda Joy Myers. $16.95, 978-1-938314-02-5.
Linda Joy Myers's story of how she transcended the prisons of her
childhood by seeking—and offering—forgiveness for her family's
sins.

Loveyoubye: Holding Fast, Letting Go, And Then There's The Dog by
Rossandra White. $16.95, 978-1-938314-50-6. A soul-searching
memoir detailing the painful, but ultimately liberating,
disintegration of a twenty-five-year marriage.

Peanut Butter and Naan: Stories of an American Mom in the Far East
by Jennifer Magnuson. $16.95, 978-1-63152-911-5. The hilarious
tale of what happened when Jennifer Magnuson moved her family
of seven from Nashville to India in an effort to shake things up—
and got more than she bargained for.

Splitting the Difference: A Heart-Shaped Memoir by Tré Miller-
Rodríguez. $19.95, 978-1-938314-20-9. When 34-year-old Tré
Miller-Rodríguez's husband dies suddenly from a heart attack, her
grief sends her on an unexpected journey that culminates in a
reunion with the biological daughter she gave up at 18.

*Pregnant Pause: A Leg to Stand On: An Amputee's Walk into
Motherhood* by Colleen Haggerty. $16.95, 978-1-63152-923-8.
Haggerty's candid story of how she overcame the pain of losing a
leg at seventeen—and of terminating two pregnancies as a young
woman—and went on to become a mother, despite her fears.

Dearest Ones at Home: Clara Taylor's Letters from Russia, 1917-1919
edited by Katrina Maloney and Patricia Maloney. Clara Taylor's
detailed, delightful letters documenting her two years in Russia
teaching factory girls self-sufficiency skills—right in the middle of
World War I.